The Devil Is in the Details

To John (The Big Boss Man):

Happy Birthday and thanks for taking an interest in my ideas!

Ellis Washington
March 5, 1999

The Devil Is in the Details

ESSAYS ON LAW, RACE, POLITICS, AND RELIGION

Ellisandro Washington

VANTAGE PRESS
New York

Material in chapters 5 and 6 originally published in *The Social Critic Journal* (Spring, 1997).
Chapter 7 originally published in *The Social Critic Journal* (Nov./Dec. 1996).
Material from *Los Angeles Times*. Copyright 1990. Reprinted by permission.
Material from the *Michigan Chronicle* reprinted from the Michigan Chronicle Newspaper Publishing Company.
Material from *The End of Racism* reprinted with permission of Simon & Schuster.

FIRST EDITION

All rights reserved, including the right of reproduction in whole or in part in any form.

Copyright © 1999 by Ellisandro Washington

Published by Vantage Press, Inc.
516 West 34th Street, New York, New York 10001

Manufactured in the United States of America
ISBN: 0-533-12690-8

Library of Congress Catalog Card No.: 98-90055

0 9 8 7 6 5 4 3 2 1

To my darling wife,

Evelyn

and to my baby son,

Stone

both precious gifts from God

Contents

Foreword   ix
Introduction   xxi
Preface   xxvii
Acknowledgments   xxxiii

Essays
1. "black" or "Black": A Plea for Legitimacy in Legal Scholarship   3
2. Racial Designations in the Bible   19
3. Arguments Against Racial Capitalization Addressed and Refuted   25
4. Liberal Law and the Scientific Mythology of Evolution: McLean v. Arkansas Board of Education   44
5. The Sophistry of Positive Law in Constitutional Jurisprudence   61
6. Constitutional Crisis   86
7. Seeking to Separate the Inseparable
   The Myth of Separation: What Is the Correct Relationship between Church and State by David Barton   101
8. Speaking Coherently, Honestly, and Freely about Race: *The End of Racism* by Dinesh D'Souza
   Part 1: Racism Mythology vs. Black Pathology   117
9. Part 2: Black Pathology   146

Foreword

The author, Ellisandro Washington, makes an outstanding and original contribution to legal scholarship by his thought-provoking work, *The Devil Is in The Details*. A stylistic departure from dry recitation of "law" intellectual vigor in what is offered; that vigor will stimulate considerable discussion amongst conservative, moderate and liberal theorists.

Clearly well-grounded in law, religion, political theory, philosophy, etc., the author expertly meshes seemingly disparate social and legal histories with a contemporary examination of "race." Avoiding the redundancy and politically correct preachment about the latter subject, the author stimulates the reader to search for potential and de facto linkages between each thesis adroitly woven into his book.

It is no mean challenge for an author to successfully marry the thesis of this book with race. This remains a volatile subject worldwide, and, indeed, evokes angry and spirited debate, argument, diatribe, in America. So much so when a California public school district recently (1997) explored the possibility of recognizing "Ebonics" as a "learning bridge" for families and children employing this linguistic maze, for those unfamiliar with its specific rules of usage, an often race-tinged vituperative battle evolved in America, and in other countries.

Ellis Washington discussed whether the word "black" is appropriately used as either a noun or proper noun, when referring to African Americans. In a controversial tack guaranteed to provide dialogue in various social, political, educational et al., camps, he discourses about Dinesh D. Souza's *The End* of Racism (1995). His methodology invites long-view historic examination.

Professor Lani Guinier who joins the Harvard University Law School faculty in September 1998, and those of her point of view, should remind Dinesh D. Souza of W.E.B. Dubois' treatise:

> After the Egyptian and Indian, the Greek and Roman, the Teuton and Mongolian, the Negro is a sort of seventh son, born with a veil, and gifted with second-sight in the American world—a world which yields him no true self-consciousness, but only lets him see himself through the revelation of the other world. It is a peculiar sensation, this double-consciousness, this sense of always looking at one's self through the eyes of others . . . One ever feels his two-ness—an American, a Negro: two souls, two un-reconciled strivings; two warring ideals in one dark body . . . The history of the American Negro is the history of this strife—this longing to attain self-consciousness manhood, to merge his double self into a better and truer self. In this merging, he wishes neither of the older selves to be lost. (Souls of Black Folk, 1903)

From the psychiatric school of thought, Grier and Cobbs in their legendary work, *Black Rage*, as well as their fellow psychiatrist, Frantz Fanon: *Negro and Language in Black Skin, White Masks,* the author adds dry kindling to this already torrid fire of linguistic, class, race-related debate and inquiry.

The author pays appropriate attention to the fact that identifiable departures in myriad fashion exist in a complex, literate, dynamic society. That generation, kinship-familial, community mores/folkways are each reciprocally wed to define the *"You and I confondre"* (confusion-funk). On the converse, *confluence* (healthy social intercourse) according to the author, is in large part predicated upon cross-racial/cultural mutual knowledge and respect. He nudges the reader toward envisioning, to a large degree, appreciation for social descriptors beyond *Noir, homme de couleur. ("Negroes.")*

For those of us known for our multiple generations' scholarly publications in sociology, diversity, history, psychology, law, Ellis Washington's intellectual foray into what is most times, *ca be casse rien (not up to much)*, racial discourse is transformed into *une noce a' tout casser (a rare jollification)*.

Thus, the reader is spared gauche *larmoyant* (lachrymose-whining). This is, of course, all too frequently employed as an apologetic crutch for standardized test differentials, along lines of race and ethnicity. Serendipity is replaced by hard-core "left-brain function."

Washington's deft *eclaricissment* (elucidation) of emotion-ladened discourse is a loud *scholarly* shout *(un grand e'clat de voix)*. Accomplishing this feat in the jurisprudence realm serves as further testimony to the author's readiness to become my colleague in academia. Surely, any law faculty would be impressed with his interdisciplinary syncretism.

Legal analyses proffered by Ellis Washington clearly reflect his awareness that sociology theory studies the "divergence and coherence" which constitute social facilitation; significantly involves a confrontation betwixt "I and You and We and They." This also encapsulates divergent emergents juxtaposed to methodologies employed to attain institutional (or personal) ends, by non-traditional means.

Bringing synthesis and clarity out of such a historic intellectual quagmire is the mark of the pure thinker. It is most refreshing to reflect upon my thirty year tenure as Ellis' mentor, professor; someone constantly challenging his reality assumptions. It is now affirmed that this author not only thinks and reasons for himself, he does not bow to the trite—politically correct camp.

This display of scholarly integrity; a willingness to employ skilled divergent exploration and thinking, again, is what the gifted professor-researcher is made of. Ellis is also a superior law professor find.

The author has demonstrably devoted a considerable sum of quality time copiously pondering his philosophical interpretation of the Constitution. He envisions, essentially, two choices: (1) *Originalism*—not revisionist, and (2) *Positivism*—rejecting strict Constitutional interpretation as set forth by the Framers—interpreting/consigning Constitutional interpretation, influenced by contemporary mores and social change dynamics.

Predictably, during intellectual discussions concerning the very philosophical foundations of education, discussants steeped in the evolution of the U.S. Constitution; the de facto meaning of "separation of powers" do battle with the positivists. Such is the fervor and tenure of such debate and discussion, *Marbury v. Madison,* is often invoked:

> Chief Justice Marshall attacked the Judicature Act of 1789. Justice Marshall's dissent from the opinion of Chief Justice Ellsworth, who served as prior Court Chief Justice to Mr. Marshall, is a perfect example of how the Positivist would seek to declare unconstitutional, thus subvert and over-ride actual language in the U.S. Constitution.
>
> Mr. Marshall alleged that President George Washington, Justice James Madison, the "father of the Constitution" failed to comprehend the meaning or intent of the Constitution, albeit, it was their conjoint work product. Mr. Madison—as today's revisionists are accused of doing—liberally interpretating the Constitution in an attempt to limit Congress' powers. Mr. Madison sought to institutionalize the notion that Congress was enjoined from adding original jurisdiction in mandamus proceedings. While Congress may not suspend the Court's appellate power under the Constitution, this does not prevent Congress' expansion of same.

Ellis Washington correctly admonishes the reader of the inherent dangers of the unilateral (and inaccurate) reinterpretation of the literal language and meaning of the U.S. Constitution. One may wish to refer to Eakin v. Aaub, 12 S.&R. 330, 344-58 (1825) and rely upon Pennsylvania's Supreme Court Justice Gibson's offerings pursuant to John Marshall's holding which examined Justice John Marshall's posit in support of judicial review.

Justice Marshall held that (Art. IIII, Sec. 2) of the Constitution provides that the Supreme Court *shall* have appellate jurisdiction, *only*; but the U.S. Congress has no statutory, political, inherent, or any other right to *invoke* original jurisdiction in *mandamus* actions. This, of course, is fallacious:

> The Constitution confers appellate power. This further means that the Congress may not vacate/quash that power. However, the Congress is not enjoined from making amendments as proscribed by way of well articulated, and formal legislative processes. Ellis Washington's treatment of the relative worth of the traditional v. activist law is encompassed quite well in the *Marbury v. Madison* discussion.

This author 'opens many doors' in his book. He offers concrete examples as understandings as to the dangers of individuals and societies disbanding various forms of "constitutions" in "expediency." The case is made sharper in his references to Adolph Hitler.

> Adolph Hitler suspended habeas corpus in order to "legitimize" his brutal, murderous rape of Germany, non-Germans, diverse ethnics, and those Hitler considered perverts or non-essential "imperfects."

In Professor Sidney M. Bolkosky's outstanding book: *The Distorted Image, German Jewish Perceptions of Germans and Germany, 1918–1935,* Elsevier Scientific Publishing Co., Inc., 1975, 52 Vanderbilt Avenue, New York, N.Y. 10017, Bolkowsky discussed how the Nazi movement involved "the synthesis" of the "oneness" of Deutschtum and Judentum.

Bolkowsky reports how in "almost every publication," definitions of German and Jewish were omnipresent; they were juxtaposed in "argumentative Festschrifen on the position of Jews in Germany or the 'Jewish Question.' " (Pg. 49) Clearly, the intent was to separate Jews and Germans; force the "majority" German population to purge itself from Jews who held loyalty to Germany as many saw themselves as Jews and Germans, simultaneously and loyal to Germany, religion aside.

Ellis Washington, from a different perspective, discussed separation. However, he effectively correlates the bifurcation of a peoples from traditional law as set forth by the Framers of the Constitution, to the grotesque machinations of Hitler, the madman. A psychotic cloaking and hiding himself within a shroud of something called "positive law." This "positive law" operates from a philosophy of "He who is sovereign, rules!" It also permits the most powerful to throw out, re-interpret, or create wholly new, non-existing laws in order to predict outcomes more consistently.

There is the tacit understanding that in the case of John Marshall, his was a self-serving agenda. Those responsible for his judicial ascription were at odds with the *Republican Judiciary Repeal Act (of 1782).* Marshall had good cause to fear impeachment should he, by way of mandamus, have ruled this Act as unconstitutional.

Marhsall's cohorts—Federalists all—stood to be thrown from offices essentially conferred them by a soon to adjourn Congress. Engaging in the sophism the author discusses in this book, Marshall seemed ripe to 'plea bargain' away powers inherent in his Court position. This cowardly quid pro quo smacks at the very heart of the author's arguments in this instant context.

Justice Marshall was prepared to insulate himself against impeachment by the self-denuding of his awesome office and powers. Thus, Ellis Washington is correct when he admonishes that the Constitution can not be treated as an old television game show name, "Let's make a deal."

The author does not attempt to mask his disdain for the activist-jurist. (S)he (the activist jurist) can expect to clash with the "strict constitution" jurist. Ellis Washington accurately comports that regardless to the political ideology of either 'camp,' it should be expected that both will consider themselves on the 'right side' of the U.S. Constitution.

Given the advent of *Miranda,* it would be a formidable burden to disprove the value of the Court's activism which requires arresting officers or those interviewing a potential arrest target to give immediate warning that whatever (s)he says can and will be used against said party in a court of law. The Framers did not incorporate this protection into the original Document because of prevailing mores at the time. Thus, the Court is not inflexible.

Of course, there is recurrent energy for change in how the U.S. Constitution is interpreted, and how the U.S. Supreme Court upholds or modifies various civil rights protections. A sore bone of contention was and remains "Stop and Frisk Laws." Clearly a Fourth Amendment issue, the Court allows reasonable searches. This is reassuring to the "traditionalist."

Mindful of Stoner v. California, 376 U.S. 483. 11 L.Ed/2nd 856. 84 S.Ct.889 (1964), based on our discussions of this case, the author and I agree with the Court's ruling (Harlan, J., sole dissenter):

> While the Court has a healthy concern for public safety, it is well-established that the Court is mindful of the right to individual freedoms under the Fourth Amendment. In *Stover v. California,* a hotel clerk admitted police officers, sans search or

arrest warrant to the room of a defendant. Remanded on appeal, it was affirmed that this act violated the rights of the complainant.

Further reinforcing of the author's trust in traditional interpretation of the U.S. Constitution, there are the cases of:

Chapman v. United States, 365 U.S.610, 81 S.Ct.776, 5 L.Ed.2nd 828, and McDonald v. United States, 335 U.S. 451, 69 S.Ct. 191, 93 L.Ed. 153. In both cases, someone hired to manage the living quarters of the complainants, allowed the improper search of premises rented by the former. Adjudged as improper searches and seizures, these and many similar cases were reversed by the Court.

The traditionalist has confidence that under strict U.S. Constitution interpretation, we in America can rely upon the Court to protect people from abuses typically commonplace in many places outside of this country. The author conveys confidence (that) this is the "American way" on one hand, and on the other, that no "absolutes" exist under any legal system.

Attorney Washington's book is a treasure trove of provocative inquiry. In a litany of questions he poses: "Is America a racist nation? What is racism? Is the Bible the founding document of America? Is America a racist place? Were America's founding fathers racists? Can African Americans be racist? What are the main problems facing African Americans—racism, discrimination, poverty or promiscuity, ignorance, and crime?"

The reader steeped in law may use the Slaughter-House Cases, 16 Wall, 36 (chap. L1,p.737, infra) as a framework from which to consider the author's questions. In Justice Miller's majority opinion in the Slaughter-House Cases, 16 Wall (chap. 11, p. 737, infra) the jurist reported:

"The most cursory glance at these three (13th, 14th, and 15th Amendments, and the enactment of the Civil Rights Acts of 1866, 1870, 1871, and 1875) discloses a unity of purpose, when taken in connection with the history of the times, which cannot fail to have an important bearing on any question of doubt concerning their true meaning. Nor can such doubts, when any reasonably exist, be safely and rationally solved without a reference to that history.

In that struggle slavery, as a legalized social relation, perished. The proclamation of President Lincoln expressed an accomplished fact as to a large portion of the insurrectionary districts, when declared slavery abolished in them all."

Slavery, an American institution, complete with Black Code Laws, the Chief Justice Taney landmark decision holding that African slave Dred Scott was only three fifths of a man, and thus not protected by the U.S. Constitution. Dred Scott, believing he had safely escaped slavery by running away to Maryland, a "free state" was, like most African slaves dehumanized and brainwashed by the very Bible the author makes reference to.

Using revisionist and selective passages as "enslaving justification," the slave-owners took great license with actual Biblical passages, or concocted non-existing passages. They read to slaves, telling them that "God" considered a hard-working, obedient slave to be a "good slave" destined for admission to Heaven. By the same token it was illegal for slaves to know how to read. Following slavery, by means of a separate and unequal school system freed-persons had neither physical plant, school books, supplies, or nurturing appropriate to compete on equal footing with the sons and daughters of their previous owners.

Despite this disparate life's chances ascription, in my own research: *Black Businesses Before, During, and After Slavery,* I documented multi-state evidence that many thousand

African Americans became highly successful business operators, educators, inventors, bankers, insurance company founders and operators, publishing giants, community developers, etc. in a dominant White *economy*. That *was* and *remains* tremendous *"power."*

Ellis Washington, unlike all too few in today's society, *is* aware of fact that (even) before and during slavery, the African American rendered moot the myth of African Americans being socially and psychologically retarded, as a racial group. Regardless, there remains a troublesome percentage of perhaps well-meaning types who postulate that African Americans cannot be racists because they have no "power." This, of course, infers the denial of the existence of highly successful African American individual businesses, corporations, industries, etc. Or, for that matter, even military command-level generals, admirals, chiefs of staffs, U.S. Presidential Cabinet members, et al.

While this book does not devote a tremendous amount of time performing social-historical autopsy upon the Fourteenth Amendment, commonly known as the "Ku Klux Klan Act," a good foundation is laid to explore this "conquered province" theory which was a U.S. Congress cornerstone, in protraction, much after the Civil War:

> In 1871, Congress created amendments (16 Stat. 433) to the 1870 Fifteenth Amendment, ratified in 1870. This action effective gave enforcement powers of serious proportion to the Fourteenth Amendment. With this, civil and criminal liabilities existed for those engaging in racial discrimination. The Civil Rights Act of 1875, 18 Stat. 335, encompassed, inter alia, the same public accommodations stanchions used by Mrs. Rosa Parks to trigger what is euphemistically called, "The Civil Rights Movement."

It makes sense, therefore, that the author poses the several race-related questions. And that he takes time to dispassionately discuss "race" as he so objectively does in his book.

This book is guaranteed to cause significant scholarly discussion along cross-academic and discipline lines. Because of this, Attorney Ellis Washington has made a vital intellectual contribution to society, and provided a blueprint for how we may productively examine serious issues confronting a number of countries, including America, at this very juncture.

FULL PROFESSOR, CLOYZELLE K. D. JONES
THE UNIVERSITY OF MICHIGAN
PRESIDENT, NATIONAL URBAN EDUCATION
ASSOCIATION, INC.
EDITOR

Introduction

I first read Ellis Washington's work some two years ago while perusing articles for possible publication in my journal, *The Social Critic*. Although at that time I had been publishing for over a year, I had not published a single piece by a Black author. This was due not to any conscious or unconscious racial bias on my part, but was simply the result of no Black authors having submitted their work. As I read his article "On the Sophistry of Positive Legal Theory," I knew Washington was a rare find. Here, at last, was an author with the firsthand knowledge and expertise to address such varied and complex issues as race, law, politics, and religion with the obloquy-free objectivity of the true scholar. At the same time, Washington writes with genuine wit and engaging *élan*.

With the publication of this, his first book, Washington has taken a major step forward in his desire to "speak coherently, honestly and freely" on these four themes. He also takes his place among the influential group of Black conservative scholars currently changing the temper of American intellectual discourse. Just as Thomas Sowell refuses to play the "race card" in economics, Ellis Washington pulls no punches in his analysis of the anti-God politics of the Left and their destructive influence on Black Americans—indeed, on *all* Americans.

In this age of pervasive "politically correct" dogma, the ideas Washington espouses in *The Devil Is in the Details* are bound to raise eyebrows. And this is as it should be. After all, as Epicurus said: "Skillful pilots gain their reputation from storms and tempests." "Playing it safe" with such issues would result in just another in a long line of forgettable books that sacrifice frank discussion for a "feel good" message. Now, more than ever, America needs an honest debate on race, law, politics and religion.

Over the past thirty years, a substantial number of Hispanic- and Asian-Americans have embraced political conservatism. Only more recently have a significant number of Black Americans come to view conservatism, broadly defined, as consistent with their world view, and begun to recognize, with Burke, that government is "a contrivance of human wisdom to provide for human *wants*"—and the more that is provided, the greater the wants. Black businesspeople and professionals (the so-called "Black *bourgeoise*") are especially cognizant of the benefits, both individual and collective, that accrue from conservative social policies. Black conservatism is unquestionably an increasingly influential movement in American politics.

To the chagrin of liberal social theorists and activists, Black Americans' moral conservatism has survived this group's rise in socioeconomic status. The *quid pro quo* that liberals expected for their work in the civil rights movement never materialized. This was due not to ingratitude on the part of Black Americans, but, rather, from a growing sense that modern liberalism is in many ways contrary to Black Americans' most deeply held moral and religious convictions. Indeed, I think it is fair to say that Black conservatism represents a sleeping giant that threatens to awaken as the differences between the beliefs of most Black Americans and those of the liberal, largely white, "cultural elite" on such issues as special homosexual rights, radical feminism, religious intolerance, the assault on the traditional family, out-of-wedlock births, and etc., become more evident. These are issues that threaten the very existence of our republic, and Black Americans understand this threat at least as well as other Americans.

Modern liberalism is in many ways a reaction against the natural law tradition of which, historically, Black Americans have been among the staunchest advocates. Thus, Washington's work is doubly relevant: not only are his ideas on law, race, politics, and religion important in their own right, but he is an eloquent expositor of the beliefs of a significant number of Black Americans who refuse to be pigeonholed politically, morally, or intellectually. This bears saying because Black Americans are commonly portrayed in the popular media as belonging to a monolithic group that has neither the political will nor sophistication to participate responsibly in shaping America's future.

As an attorney and legal scholar, Washington is adept at exposing the fallacies of positive and sociological legal theory. Adopting a natural law stance, he castigates the legal theories used to justify the atrocities committed by the Nazis in World War II. As Washington rightly observes, the Nuremberg prosecutors resorted to natural law precepts in order to convict the war criminals. Thus, he makes clear the important distinction between *malum prohibitum* and natural law's *malum in se*. It is precisely this distinction that is so conspicuously absent from contemporary American jurisprudence.

It is quite true that one of modern liberalism's greatest achievements—in my view its *only* great achievement—was to expedite the snaillike progress of American minority group rights. Through their vocal—at times *physical*—support of both the Civil Rights Act of 1964 and the Voting Rights Act of 1965, White liberals helped to improve the lives of millions of Americans of color. It would be a mistake, however, to suppose that because Black Americans and White liberals were fighting the same good fight a generation ago, that they are now joined at the hip politically. Ultimately, the "politically correct" Procrustean bed into which liberals have tried to frame the Black experience in America has shown itself to be one-dimensional, concentrating more on the "politics of blackness" than on this group's rich cultural heritage.

Liberal intolerance of Black conservatism is especially revealing. Note the look of betrayal on the faces of White liberals when confronted by conservative Blacks. Note, too, the liberal aversion to treating racial minorities as individuals. Furthermore, the present liberal concern for "group rights" over individual rights is antithetical to Martin Luther King Jr.'s belief that people ought be judged "not by the color of their skin, but by the content of their character." One wonders what Dr. King would have thought of the liberal turn toward "race politics."

We now see the strange spectacle of White liberals accusing conservative Blacks of being "confused" or "uninformed" as to the politics they *should* support. Through the force of his ideas, Washington rebuffs this condescending paternalism. As a friend of mine, who is also Black and a priest, explained to me after a group of White liberals from nearby Berkeley demanded he change the decor of the church in which he serves to reflect their own vision of Black racial "authenticity," "They know nothing of me, nor of these parishioners. To them, everything is a *political statement.*" I doubt that this is what W. E. B. DuBois anticipated when he presaged the twentieth-century debate on race.

Underlying Washington's views on politics, race, and law is a deeply held Christian faith. I know from reading his work and from our personal conversations that love of God and family serve as vital sources of strength as he tackles the controversial issues as race, law, politics, and religion. Washington is not merely a legal and social theorist—he is a good man and an exemplar to the Black conservative intellectuals who will follow him.

Finally, I must say that, to his credit, Washington has shown remarkable patience and determination in bringing this important book to print. This is a project that few attempt and far fewer see through to completion. Time will tell whether *The Devil Is in the Details* will be considered Washington's *magnum opus*; it is significant in itself, however, as his first major work.

—C. James Newlan,
Founder and Publisher of The Social Critic Journal
24 March 1998
Hayward, CA.

Preface

My first book, *The Devil Is in the Details: Essays on Law, Politics, Race, and Religion,* was originally titled: *Normative Principles in Legal Philosophy* . . . I have changed the title to make it more interesting and accessible to the general public. Furthermore, this title better conveys the thinking that led to the compilation of several past writings of mine into a single volume. The question then became—what do these various writings have in common to form a coherent text? The answer is that each piece has an *idée fixe,* a common theme if you will—taking a small fact, belief, phrase, doctrine, or philosophy that most people are familiar with and analyze how a seemingly minor, insignificant point can and does have monumental implications in our daily lives, oftentimes subverting our cherished civil liberties!

This book is actually a collection of selected writings of mine on law, race, politics, and religion, covering exactly a six-year period of time. The first essay was written February 27, 1991, and the entire book manuscript was completed February 27, 1997. This date has personal significance to me for it was the birthday of my stepfather, Melvin L. Green (a.k.a. Osei Tutu). Regrettably, my mentor and friend has recently died (October 1997), but his inspiration, support, and source materials from his small but substantive library provided me with a wealth of ideas, especially in the opening and closing chapters of the book, regarding race and racism. The first essay, " 'black' or 'Black': A Plea for Legitimacy in Legal Scholarship," comprises the first three chapters and was written as an exercise (a musical etude if you will), chronicling my experiences as an editor at the *Michigan Law Review* (1989). There I was personally confronted with the dilemma implied in the above title. This editorial experience prompted me to undertake a systematic survey of the past and current legal scholarship as well as writings of several other disciplines, to seek a better understanding of why legal scholars (and to a lesser degree other academic books, journals, and newspapers) referred to Black people in the lowercase. Interestingly, this was shortly after the time I had made my decision to go to law school while a graduate student in musicology at Harvard.

The second essay (chapter 4), "Liberal Law and the Scientific Mythology of Evolution: McLean vs. Arkansas Board of Education," was taken from a larger unpublished work titled, *Can Church and State Be Separated?: A Constitutional Analysis,* which I completed in June 1991. I have revised and adapted this work somewhat to correspond to the overall theme of this collection of writings. This essay details how radical liberalism and radical egalitarianism has perverted two once great and respected bodies of knowledge: Law and Science. It is now academic that since the 1960s these two disciplines have been shamelessly politicized and perverted by the so-called intellectual classes (i.e., professors, lawyers, judges, scientists, journalists, politicians, bureaucrats, et al.) and that theories and beliefs which were only a generation ago widely regarded as untenable, unworkable, and sophistic, (i.e., evolution, naturalism, and positive law) are now heralded as orthodoxy by these so-called guardians of our sacred intellectual canons. In this essay, I chronicle how these defenses are mounted even against an increasing amount of scientific and historical evidence that categorically refute these ideologies.

The third essay (chapters 5 and 6), is titled, "The Sophistry of Positive Law in Constitutional Jurisprudence," was originally published in the *Social Critic Journal,* Vol. 2, No. 2,

Spring 1997, titled: "On The Sophistry of Positive Legal Theory," and is a historical analysis on the philosophical foundations of the Constitution of the United States and the ongoing war of jurisprudence and separation of power conflicts between the three branches of government: legislative, executive, and judicial. In the judicial area, jurists are debating whether a document like the Constitution, written over two hundred years ago, can have *any* relevance in modern times. The quandary that the intellectual class has is this: what philosophy will we use to interpret the Constitution? We essentially have two choices: (1) Originalism, or adopting the views of the Constitution that the original Framers held; (2) Positivism, which ignores the Framers' view of the Constitution, substituting a "living" or "evolving" interpretation in accordance with the morality of the times. The latter view has been largely discredited since the 1980s; however liberals, who by in large continue to control our intellectual and law making institutions, slavishly and irrationally cling to sophistic speculations.

Chapter 7, "Seeking to Separate the Inseparable," is a review essay of David Barton's *The Myth of Separation* (1992). This review was previously published in the journal *The Social Critic,* Vol. 1, No. 5, Nov./Dec. 1996, titled: "The Myth of Separation: What Is the Correct Relationship between Church and State?" This chapter is a companion piece to the previous essay and specifically addresses how modern-day Courts have substituted the biblical principles of *natural law* that the original Framers of the Constitution held paramount, and substituted a pagan, secular, humanistic, and counterfeit philosophy: *positive law*—he who is sovereign rules! Recent history has also vindicated natural law and castigated positive law for during the years leading up to World War II and its aftermath, it was the naked aggression, brute force, and counter-logic of positive law that gave the world Stalin's maniacal purges of 1936–37, and his subsequent Gulag Archipelago in

Russia; Chinese Premier, Mao Tse-tung's reckless and ultimately genocidal experiments in collective farming ironically called "The Great Leap Forward" in the early 1950s; and Adolph Hitler's Holocaust in Germany. Each of these recent historical events was deeply steeped in the rhetoric and philosophy of positive law and several other related naturalistic philosophies and supplied the ideological justification for the senseless deaths of 30 million Russians, 30 million Chinese peasants, 6 1/2 million Jews respectively, as well as hundreds of thousands of Gypsies, homosexuals, the handicapped, the mentally impaired, and "enemies of the state."

Chapters 8 and 9 are the only new material in this book (completed February 24, 1997) and consist of an extended review essay in two parts on Dinesh D'Souza's *The End of Racism* (1995). Here I systematically explore D'Souza's "radical" beliefs about race and racism, using copious amounts of original text, interspersed with my general narrative, which expands and expounds upon the theses of his arguments, one of them being that racism is no longer a primary barrier to the success of African Americans but a lack of developed ability and demonstrated performance levels that are, in general, significantly lower than those of other racial groups in America.

I believe that it was the great physicist Albert Einstein who, while responding to questions regarding his newly discovered "Theory of Relativity," answered, "The devil is in the details." I understand this to mean that the formula for his theory, $E=MC^2$, seems simple on its face; however, once scientists began to do experiments based on his theorems, and systematically explored its means and ends, the true complexity and foreboding implications of this theory foreshadowed the future hellish nightmares of Hiroshima and Nagasaki a generation later, and the forty-five-year Cold War between Russia and the U.S. which carved up the world on ideological grounds—Communism vs. Democratic-Republic. The fallout of these experiments is still tragically with us today, hanging over humanity like the Sword of Damocles.

Thus, in my book, *The Devil Is in the Details,* seemingly minor or insignificant points like: Should the word *black* be capitalized in print when it refers to race? Should creation science be given "equal time" in the public schools along with evolution? Is evolution any longer a viable scientific explanation for the origins of life given a crescendo of scientific evidence that proves evolution impossible? If not, why is evolution still thought as fact? And why are other scientific explanations of the origins of life so vigorously opposed by the scientific community and liberal special interest groups and given the imprimatur of legal sanction by an activist judiciary? Is the judicially created doctrine *separation of church and state* rooted in the Constitution? Is the Constitution a natural law document? And if so, will the application of positive law principles to the Constitution be feasible? In a "Christian nation," as the Supreme Court said of America, *can* church and state be separate? What should the response of the American public be to politicians and others in authority who try to remove all Judeo-Christian influence from the public marketplace? Is the Bible the founding document of America? Should men like Washington, Jefferson, and Mason be revered as heroes or reviled as hypocrites because they owned slaves while espousing the republican principle that "all men are created equal"? What is racism? Is America a racist nation? Were America's founding fathers racists? Can African Americans be racists? What are the main problems facing African Americans?—Racism, discrimination, poverty or promiscuity, ignorance, crime? These and many other questions are addressed and answered in the following collection of essays. It is hoped that the reader will find this book as interesting and enjoyable as the author found writing it.

Chicago, IL
March 4, 1997

Acknowledgments

From the behaviorists point of view, the individual adult is, to a large degree, the sum total of his environment. The growing child is fortunate if they have a mother such as my own Mom, Joan. She combined consistent love, guidance, encouragement, age appropriate structure; exposed me to the arts, academic challenges, and social responsibility. In collaboration with her surrogate brother, Dr. Cloyzelle K.D. Jones, my lifelong mentor and teacher, I was influenced by their mutually-shared talents as musicians (my mother sang classics), and Dr. Jones' professional musicianship and acclaimed oil painting/sculpturing. Both stimulated me academically, and served as realistic role models, by becoming successful members of the academic community.

To Arthur R. LaBrew, musicologist, friend, mentor, teacher, and founder of the Michigan Music Research Center (Detroit, MI) for taking me under his tutelage eleven years ago and for being such a splendid example of academic rigor, integrity, and assiduousness.

To Dr. Kenneth Boa, Biblical scholar, teacher, author, and founder of Trinity Publishers and Reflections Ministry (Atlanta, GA).

To Melvin L. Green (a.k.a. Osei Tutu), deceased. A tireless friend, wellspring of knowledge, and my stepfather, whom I miss exceedingly.

To Dean David Meltz of John Marshall Law School (Atlanta, GA), for encouraging the development of my legal research and writing skills, fostering critical thinking, and exposing me to the works of Frederick Hayek, Morton Friedman, and Ayn Rand. To Dean D'Agostino for his moral support and interest in my ideas.

To Bishop T.D. Jakes, Senior Pastor of The Potter's House Church and founder of T.D. Jakes Ministries, Dallas, Texas. Your sermon series: "The Puppetmaster," "Leftovers," "Seven Steps to a Turn Around," " Man Power Vols. I, II and III," as well as many other tapes, brought me out of a self-defeating, negative attitude of despondency because of repeated failures at passing the bar exam in 1994. Your messages of self-help made me realize that the seeds of greatness were in me—I just had to birth it out!

Last, but not least, my sister, Sonya, my sister-in-law, Yemoja, fellow author, Mother Julia Green, Antioch C.O.G.I.C. (Detroit, MI), and my dear wife, Evelyn, for all your love and support during the hard times.

The Devil Is in the Details

Essays

1

"black" or "Black": A Plea for Legitimacy in Legal Scholarship

February 27, 1991
We eschew the recital of our credenda.[1]
—William F. Buckley

[Black should not be regarded] as merely a color of skin pigmentation, but as a heritage, an experience, a cultural and personal identity.[2]
—Katherine MacKinnon

Introduction

The subject of legitimizing *Black* Americans in print generally and in legal scholarship specifically, by utilizing the uppercase, is not without precedent. This grammatical jot has tremendous implications in aiding or hindering the African American in their search for equal treatment under the law by removing from them this second-class treatment of their race in print. Therefore, the thesis of this Essay is an earnest plea to legal scholarship community to lead the way by no longer referring to African Americans in print as *black,* in the lowercase, but as *Black,* a capitalized proper noun. To underscore this point, throughout this Essay I have italicized the words *Black* and *White* whenever they refer to racial designation, and their antecedents—Colored, Negro, Afro-American, and African American. By accepting my theses law scholars will send an urgently viable message to the entire academic community that the delineation of *black*, in the lowercase, will no longer be acceptable in legal scholarship.

Law professor Kimberly Williams Crenshaw's law review article served as a catalyst in undertaking my own survey of the literature to find examples of racial discrimination in legal scholarship.[3] At the beginning of her article, she states that she "shall use "African-American" and *"Black"* interchangeably. When using *"Black,"* I shall use an upper-case "B" to reflect my view that *Blacks,* like Asians, Latinos, and other "minorities," constitute a specific cultural group and, as such, require denotation as a proper noun. In a similar vein, feminist law professor Katherine MacKinnon wrote that *"Black"* should not be regarded "as merely a color of skin pigmentation, but as a heritage, an experience, a cultural and personal identity, the meaning of which becomes specifically stigmatic and/or glorious and/or ordinary under specific social conditions."[4] The naming of Americans of African descent has had political overtones throughout history. W. E. B. Dubois has noted:

> The "N" in Negro was always capitalized until, in defense of slavery, the use of the lower [*sic*] case "n" became the custom in "recognition" of Blacks' status as property; that the usage was defended as a "description of the color of a people;" and that the capitalization of other ethnic and national origin designations made the failure to capitalize "Negro" an insult.[5]

Crenshaw further states:

> African-American is now preferred by some because it is both culturally more specific and historically more expansive than the traditional terms that narrowly categorize us as America's "other" and that the embrace of the self-definition "African-

American" can symbolize the ongoing effort to break free of the subordinate self-identity brought about by exclusive reference to a white norm.[6]

In America, the official manual of style for the majority of all law reviews and law journals is called *A Uniform System of Citation*. Under the title *Capitalization,* the following rule is cited:

Capitalized nouns referring to people or groups only when they identify specific **persons,** officials, **groups,** government offices, or government bodies.[7]

The rule plainly states to capitalize persons and groups. *Blacks* and *Whites* are racial designations no different than Indian, Hispanic, Hungarian, or Irish. Why then have *law review* editorial boards unilaterally ignored their own rules concerning racial delineation is beyond the pale? The irony here is self-evident—the usage of the lowercase "b" to represent *Black* Americans, especially in the context of civil rights, civil liberties, and anti-discrimination law scholarship, not only is grammatically incorrect, but scholastically hypocritical, personally insulting, and ultimately inimical to eliminating racist and unfair discriminatory practices against *Black* people in America.

The use of the word *black* in legal scholarship to identify the *Black* American race is not only demeaning, but the word lacks significance and legitimacy on its face because it is understood by the reader as merely an adjective masquerading as a proper noun. The use of the word *black,* whether on a conscious or unconscious level, is immediately viewed by the reader as less significant because it is used in the lowercase. The words *legitimacy* and *significance* will frequently occur throughout this Essay because I wish to draw the parallel between the dichotomy—importance = capitalization and insignificance = lowercase, implicit throughout the English language. Furthermore, it will be stated that by capitalizing the word *Black* in legal scholarship, not only does one imbue equality, significance, and legitimacy to this particular word, but more importantly, to the entire race of people by which the word, *Black,* specifically describes. The use of the word *Black* as a proper noun or a proper adjective in delineating race makes capitalization imperative for grammatical reasons. For example, *Warriner's Handbook of English* states that "all proper nouns and proper adjectives should be capitalized" and "all organizations, institutions, business products, special events, calendar items, *races,* and religions" should always be capitalized. In Lewis's *Correct Spelling Made Easy,* the author writes that the correct spelling for *Negro* should always begin with a capital.[8] Although the previous examples refer to the anachronistic term, *Negro,* this is simply the Spanish word for "black" or "dark." In tracing the etymological origins of *Negro, The Reader's Digest Great Encyclopedia Dictionary* states that the Latin root word for *Negro* is *Niger,* taken from the great West African river which is very dark and muddy.[9] Secondly, another well-known source that supports my thesis is the Bible. The Bible always identifies its racial groups (including progenitors of the *Black* or *Negro* race) with a capital befitting a proper noun. For example, in Numbers 12:1, "And Miriam and Aaron spake against Moses because of the *Ethiopian* woman whom he had married: for he had married an *Ethiopian* woman." In the Bible, "Ethiopian" is a synonym for "Cushite" or the descendants of Cush, the Biblical progenitor of the *Black* race. A more in-depth discussion on the Biblical support of this thesis will be cited later in this Essay.[10] Thirdly, in my review of the legal scholarship literature as noted earlier, the law review manual of legal citation clearly states that all references to race or racial groups must be capitalized.[11] Unfortunately, many of our law dictionaries subscribe to the faulty traditional spelling, referring to *Black* Americans with the lowercase *b*. In Brian Garner's *A Dictionary of Modern Legal Usage,* the following entry for *black* is given:

> black; Black; Negro; Afro-American. Currently it is best to use *black*(lowercase), n. & adj. E.g., "In *Jones v. Alfred H. Mayer Co.*, the complaint charged a refusal to sell petitioner a home because he was *black.*"[12]

In *Black's Law Dictionary,* the most widely used and respected law dictionary in America, has no citation for either *Black, African American,* or *Negro* are found, but it does contain an entry for "*colored*"—quoted in full it states:

> Colored. By common usage in America, this term, in such phrases as "colored persons," "the colored race," "colored men," and the like, is used to designate negroes or persons of the African race, including all persons of mixed blood descended from negro ancestry.[13]

This last entry is peculiar because *African Americans* haven't been referred to as *colored* for over eighty years! Looking at these two legal definitions brings up several points: (1) It is regrettable that *Black's Law Dictionary,* one of the most highly regarded and widely used in the legal field, didn't contain the terms *Negro, Black, African American,* or *Afro-American,* the former being used in literature as far back as 1501, when the Portuguese and Spanish first began exporting slaves from Africa and bringing them to the New World; the other two terms, *Black* and *Afro American,* gaining usage in literature about 1960 and 1970 respectively. (2) What is more disappointing is that *Black's Law Dictionary* chose to include the archaic term "*colored,*" which, although sometimes used in judicial opinions before 1940, is both irrelevant and offensive in current legal scholarship, or for that matter in any other type of serious writing. *Garner's Dictionary,* on the other hand, includes the terms—*black, Negro,* and *Afro-American.* It also cites the term *Black* in the uppercase as a viable delineation of race, but one which is currently rejected by the legal community. This is true, but unfortunately, neither Garner nor any of his sources have offered any reason *why* capitalizing the word *Black* when referring to *Black* people is rejected by the legal community or why it is "currently best to use *black*". Finally, I think that it would send a strong, clear message in fighting against racial discrimination in print if America's most used and trusted legal dictionary, would revise it's article regarding *"colored"* people to include the terms *Afro-American, Black,* and *African American.* These are clear examples of racial discrimination in legal scholarship and are an unnecessary injustice as well as a blatant insult to all *Black* people in America. Furthermore, in American legal scholarship, every race is identified by their national origin and when necessary, the word "American" is added as a suffix (i.e., *Jewish, Jewish American; Italian, Italian American; German, German American*). The lone exception to this rule is the racial designation, *black* American.

From the origins of slavery in America to the 1950's, *Black* people were most frequently referred to as: *Africans, darkies, Nigger, colored, Negro, Black,* and *Afro-American* in addition to many other epithets too numerous and unnecessary to mention here. As mentioned by DuBois in the beginning of this Essay, the word *Negro* was usually referred to in the uppercase prior to the 1900's. The term *Afro-American* was especially prominent in print during the 1960's and 1970's when the prefix *afro* (presumably derived from *Afri*, as in African, or possibly derived from "natural," which was a hairstyle that was in vogue during the same period when *Black* people wore their hair in a large bushy, rounded shape) was used. The afro hairstyle represented a radical departure from hairstyles of the previous decades where *Black* people tried to soften or blend in their overt African features (primarily through hair and skin color juxtaposition by using various greases, jells, and facial creams) to more closely resemble the pure *White* ideal popularized in American movies, in advertisements, and in daily life. Ironically, the first *Black* American woman to earn a million dollars, Madame C. J. Walker, achieved her fortune manufacturing hair straightening products in the 1920's for a booming African American market after World War I. For example, one of the popular hair care devises used at that time was the "*straightening comb,*" a cast-iron comb that when heated on top of a stove and applied to the hair "straightened" it out, thus making it more manageable. Ms. Walker's company also manufactured various greases and jells specifically designed for coarse textured hair. Thus, by using the racial term Afro-American, *Black* people attempted to state in print what was simultaneously happening to them politically during the 1960's and 1970's—affirming their racial identity, and at the same time embracing their link (however precarious) to America and the lofty ideals of freedom and equality it represented to the world. In theory that was adequate for those times. However, ironically, in retrospect, the term *Afro-American* is more degrading than the term *Black* in identifying race. What other race of people are delineated by the pigmentation of *some* of their exponent's skin? ("Negro," "Black," "colored," "people of color") or even more disparaging, the texture of a *percentage* of the races' hair texture (*"Afro-American"*). Today it is ludicrous to refer to a *Black* person as an *Afro-American* because very few *Blacks* even wear the afro hairstyle. Therefore, racial discrimination in print is a lamentable absence of justice, morality, and equality under the law towards African Americans, and it must change.[14]

Concerning the question of law and morality, some may argue against the validity of "morality" in law as not constituting a permissible statutory standard in judicial decision making. For example, in a Harvard Law Review article, the author stated that "immoral did not constitute a permissible statutory standard. An opinion . . . not directly related to morals did not carry the requisite conviction."[15] The question of legality as being separate and distinct from morality is a seriously unconstitutional flawed, but popular legal doctrine. However, any law not rooted in morality is by definition immoral, and ultimately subversive and anarchical. My ideas on this topic are discussed in greater detail in the subsequent essay and book reviews.

Origins of Discontent:
Editor at the *Michigan Law Review*

In 1989, the Michigan Law Review devoted an entire volume on law review articles utilizing the literary form of legal narrative as a devise to combat racism. At the behest of law professor Richard Delgado, then at the University of Wisconsin Law School, the University of Michigan and several other *law reviews* symposiums were presented on legal narrative in April 1989.[16] The articles varied in approach and procedure in using legal narrative to combat racism at every level—Federal, State, Local. All of the articles were substantive and interesting and each author contributed significantly to making this particular volume the best selling in the history of the Michigan Law Review to date.[17]

While I was working as an editor for the Michigan Law Review during the summer of 1989, it became increasingly perplexing that every time the word *Black* appeared in a law review article I was editing, it was always in the lowercase. I worked on the August 1989 volume of this law review which contained a special edition of articles relating to the use of the literary technique, narrative, and applying it to civil rights issues, giving voice and legitimacy to minority concerns as they related to civil rights, civil liberties, and anti-discrimination law in legal scholarship. Articles were submitted by such notable civil rights legal scholars as Derrick Bell, Mari Matsuda, Patricia Williams, Richard Delgado, Kim Scheppele, Toni Massaro, David Luban, Steven L. Winter, Milner Ball, Joseph Singer, and Clark Cunningham. My primary duties included editing, research, and citation checking of the authors sources for all the entries to that volume, but I worked primarily on the Bell, Matsuda, Williams, and Delgado articles. What made my job particularly ironic was that I was editing a special volume of the law review articles devoted solely to works by leading legal scholars who were supposedly criticizing racism and discriminatory practices in the law specifically as applied to racial minorities. However, throughout their articles, these same scholars referred to African Americans with the cursory epithet *black*. Many of these scholars, whose articles we were edited at the Michigan Law Review, have had long and notable careers in civil rights, civil liberties, and anti-discrimination law scholarship, as well as being affiliated with some of the most prestigious law schools in America. To indict these scholars with deliberately slighting a certain race of people would be contradictory to the spirit and letter of their ideas. As part of my editorial duties, I then corrected what I perceived an innocent omission by capitalizing the words *Black* and *White* whenever it pertained to a person or racial group. However, my "corrections" never were realized as were my many other corrections, deletions and additions I had made in subsequent drafts of the articles I reviewed. When I made inquiry to the Editor in Chief as to why my edits weren't taken in instances of capitalizing *Black* when the word refers to race. I was informed that it was the law review board of editors that decided what final form, style, and content the articles would take, including which proper nouns would be capitalized and which would not. As mentioned earlier, most law reviews use the writing manual—*A Uniform Sys-*

tem of Citation, as a style guide for legal writing. At that time, I errantly assumed that the Review used the lowercase when addressing *Black* and *White* Americans because that was the rule according to the style manual, which was euphemistically referred to as "the Bible" for law review editors. However, in doing research for this Essay, I have since discovered that the manual *does* specifically cover this grammatical question, and the rule is that delineation of *any* racial group *should* be capitalized.[18]

Traditionally, the Harvard Law School, and particularly its law review, has set the standard for American legal scholarship for over a century. There are several reasons for this: (1) Its University (1636) and its law school (1817) and law review (1887) are the oldest and most established in America; (2) Its faculty are exemplary and respected as the foremost legal scholars in their fields; (3) Harvard University has a several billion dollar endowment; and, (4) the Harvard Law Review has some of the best offerings of legal scholarship of any law review in America. With this in mind, I reviewed the earliest editions of the Harvard Law Review to find examples of how *Black* racial groups were delineated. I then did a cursory analysis of succeeding years of the Review, noting the changes in names and spellings. In one article written in 1890, the author stated, "... separate schools for the education of *white* and *colored* children."[19] Twenty years later in 1910, another author stated that, [concubinage] "between a person of the *Caucasian,* or *white* race, and a person of the *negro,* or *black* race," a felony.[20] By the early 1940's, the word "negro" began receiving capital designation in the Harvard Law Review. For example, an author in 1940 wrote, "a more analytical survey of the law affecting the *Negro* in modern society has long been evident" and in "In *Sweat v. Painter,* petitioner, a *Negro,* was refused admission to the University of Texas Law School."[21] An author in a 1961 article wrote, "In *Williams v. Georgia,* the *Negro* petitioner had been convicted of murder by an all-white jury and sentenced to death."[22] You can see by these few examples, that the Harvard Law Review, America's premiere law review, has been inconsistent in the delineation of its's racial groups in print. Unfortunately, among law reviews and law journals, they are not alone.

"black" or "Black": Illegitimacy vs. Legitimacy

Why are there so many publications on the market—from law reviews to local newspapers, from tabloids to national news magazines, from tawdry novels to great works of literature—that single out the racial designation, *black*, as the exception to be used in the lowercase in print? In asking myself this question, I began to rationalize that perhaps most people never really thought about it, or perhaps to others, it is an insignificant matter not worthy of serious discussion. However, speaking of an entire race of people in the lowercase is a problem; a very serious one, especially when all other races are designated in the uppercase in print. Also, it became especially ironic when I read articles by noted civil rights and anti-discrimination law scholars using the diminutive form of *black* when their primary reason for writing the article was to use legal scholarship and legal narrative to fight against racism and discrimination towards racial minority groups. As I grappled with what appeared to me to be the editorial hypocrisy of the Michigan Law Review on this point, somehow, perhaps at an unconscious level, I found the use of the word *black*, when referring to race, extremely insulting. For example, in a sentence with a list of other racial/national groups, the racial designation, *black*, became particularly irksome the more I saw it in legal scholarship. For example, legal scholar Richard Burt, in a book on Jewish Justices, Brandeis, and Frankfurter titled, *Two Jewish Justices: Outcast in a Promised Land*, stated that

"... such as *blacks* or *Jews* ... for *Jews*, for *blacks*, for other minorities, for all Americans...."[23] In this passage several racial groups were cited, but *Black* Americans were singled out to be printed in the lowercase. Thus, this passage made his work less convincing to me, as a reader, in using legal scholarship to combat racial discrimination in print than I think it could have been had Burt capitalized the word *Black*. Using the capital designation would have signaled to the reader that Burt actually believed what he was writing about; that indeed he advocated equality of all races. I do not place the blame all on legal scholars, for their work must fall under the current guidelines of editorial boards prior to the book's final publication. But now is the time for scholars of law to lead the way to rectify this continued inconsistency delineating *"black"* Americans in print using the lowercase.[24]

Another way to analyze this problem is that one could interpret the words—*black/Black*— as having two distinct and separate meanings. The first term, *"black,"* being interpreted as an insignificant, cursory, inferior race of people, not worthy to be capitalized as grammar dictates all proper pronouns and proper adjectives should be.[25] The latter term, *"Black,"* could be interpreted as a racial designation worthy of equal delineation in its characterization of race in all forms of print—especially in scholarly writings. If the legal scholarship community would send a clarion call against lowercase designation of any racial group, I am convinced that other magazines, newspapers, scholarly journals, and publications of every type would follow suit. This seemingly minor point of whether *Black* people should be referred to with a capital has monumental, moral, ideological, grammatical, social, and political implications. The most expedient being that the rendering of the *Black* race in the lowercase fosters a sense of negativeness, inferiority, and unimportance to the Black race. This grammatical omission adds insult to injury on a race of people that has suffered and continues to endure untold racial, political, educational, and societal discrimination in America.[26]

According to the U.S. Bureau of Census Statistical Population Reports, African Americans make up over 12% of the U.S. population.[27] The question should then be asked: Why should such a large population of people be referred to in print in the lower case, while other less populous groups in America (i.e., Hispanics, Indians, Jews), or races with a lower gross national product (GNP) (Mexico, Sweden, Italy), or even races with a less significant role in American history to be discriminated against in print? Black people have played a pivotal role in American history from the arrival of the first African slaves in 1619 through America's Colonial, Revolutionary, Civil, and World Wars. Martin Luther King, Jr., one of the greatest intellectual minds of the twentieth century, eloquently paid homage to the contributions of his race as a primary reason for America's wealth and prosperity citing that "[b]efore the Pilgrims landed at Plymouth [Rock] we were here." King further chronicled:

> [A]bused and scorned though we may be, our destiny is tied up with America's destiny. Before the pen of Jefferson etched the majestic words of the Declaration of Independence across the pages of history, we were here. For more than two centuries our forebears labored in this country without wages; they made cotton king; they built the homes of their masters while suffering a bottomless vitality they continued to thrive and develop. If the inexpressible cruelties of slavery could not stop us, the opposition we now face will surely fail. We will win our freedom because the sacred heritage of our nation and the eternal will of God are embodied in our echoing demands.[28]

Certainly you couldn't say that the Japanese or the Chinese

had as viable an impact in American history. Neither could it be said of the Russians, Scandinavians, of even in most other European nations, that they have had a more salient position in America's history than that of *Black* Americans, however ignominious and involuntary that history may have been. Yet *Black* people are repeatedly discriminated and segregated in print to the diminutive, lowercase spelling of *black*. This spelling discriminates against *Blacks* as a race in print, and the grammatical symbolism is tantamount to putting *Black* people at the back of the bus, or to make them use segregated public facilities as in the recent past. Racial discrimination in print must change, and I propose that it change now. I hope that the legal scholarship community will take the lead in rectifying this injustice. Two of the main purposes of American law are to right that which is wrong, and to provide to all its citizens due process and equal protection under the law. Finally, it is hoped that the legal community will put an end to delineating any racial group, *Black* or *White,* in the lowercase, and to begin following the capitalization rules in its own manual, the *Uniform System of Citation,* capitalizing the racial designation, *Black,* when referring to *Black* people (individually or collectively) in print. I am convinced that this seemingly innocuous gesture will put *Black* people on an equal footing (at least in print) with all the other nations and races of the international pantheon.

Notes

1. William F. Buckley, "Agenda for the Nineties," *National Review,* February 19, 1990, at 1, col.
2. Katherine MacKinnon, "Feminism, Marxism, Method, and the State: An Agenda for Theory, 7 Signs," *Journal of Women in Culture & Society,* pp. 515–16, (1982). Cited by Kimberly Williams Crenshaw, "Race, Reform, and Retrenchment: Transformation and Legitimation

in Antidiscrimination Law," *Harvard Law Review,* 101, (1988), pp. 1331-32, note 2.
3. Crenshaw, "Race, Reform," pp. 1331-32.
4. Katherine MacKinnon, "Feminism," pp. 515-16.
5. W. E. B. Du Bois, *The Seventh Son,* Random House, New York, 1971, pp. 12-13.
6. Crenshaw, "Race, Reform," p. 1385, note 200.
7. The official law review manual of style used at most American law schools is: *A Uniform System of Citation,* Cambridge, MA, 1986, pp. 31-33. Hereinafter, *Manual.*
8. John E. Warriner, *Handbook of English,* Harcourt, Brace & World, Inc., NY, 1948, pp. 37, 39; Norman Lewis, *Correct Spelling Made Easy,* Dell Publishing Co., NY, 1963, p. 291.
9. *The Reader's Digest Great Encyclopedic Dictionary,* The Reader's Digest Assoc., Inc., 1968, pp. 906, 913.
10. All Biblical references will be taken from the authorized standard King James Version (1611).
11. *Manual,* pp. 31-33.
12. Brian Garner, *A Dictionary of Modern Legal Usage,* Oxford University Press, New York, 1987, p. 88.
13. *Black's Law Dictionary,* West Publishing Company, St. Paul, 1979.
14. "African-American or Black: What's in a Name?" *Ebony,* July, 1989, pp. 79-80.
15. "The Supreme Court, 1953 Term," *Harvard Law Review,* 68, (1954), p. 101.
16. *Michigan Law Review,* 87, (1989), p. 1139. The August 1989 volume of this law review contained a special edition of articles delivered at the University of Michigan Law School Symposium on Legal Narrative in Hutchins Hall, April of 1989. The articles related to a diversity of civil rights issues that used the literary devise of narrative to give voice and legitimacy to minority concerns as they related to civil rights, civil liberties, and antidiscrimination law in legal scholarship. The symposium was organized by Professor Richard Delgado, then professor of law at the University of Wisconsin Law School. Articles were submitted by: Derrick Bell, Mari Matsuda, Patricia Williams, Richard Delgado, Kim Lane Scheppele, Toni Massaro, David Luban, Steven Winter, Milner Ball, Joseph Singer, and Clark D. Cunningham. See Derrick Bell, *And We Are Not Saved,* Basic Books, New York, 1987, for an exemplary metaphorical treatment of antidiscrimination law in the form of narrative commentary.
17. Personal conversations with David Meyer, Editor-in-Chief of the *Michigan Law Review,* Ann Arbor, MI. September 1988-August 1989. In August, 1989, David informed me that this particular issue sold the most copies of any *Michigan Law Review* to date.

18. See *Manual,* pp. 31–33.
19. *Harvard Law Review,* 4, (1890), p. 397: "Separate schools for the education of *white* and *colored* children" (emphasis mine).
20. *Harvard Law Review,* 24, (1910), p. 68: "[Concubinage] between a person of the *Caucasian* or *white* race and a person of the *negro* or *black* race" a felony (quotation marks in original) (emphasis mine).
21. *Harvard Law Review,* 54, (1940), p. 178: "A more analytical survey of the law affecting the *Negro* in modern society has long been evident" (emphasis mine); *Harvard Law Review,* 68, (1950), p. 130: "In *Sweat v. Painter,* petitioner, a *Negro,* was refused admission to the University of Texas Law School." (footnote omitted) (emphasis mine).
22. *Harvard Law Review,* 74, (1961), pp. 1375, 1389, "In *Williams v. Georgia,* the *Negro* petitioner had been convicted of murder by an all-white jury and sentenced to death." (emphasis mine) (footnote omitted).
23. See Richard Burt, *Two Jewish Justices: Outcast in a Promised Land,* University of California Press, Berkeley, 1987, p. 3. See also, Book Review by G. Edward White of Richard Burt's, *Two Jewish Justices: Outcasts in a Promised Land, Michigan Law Review,* 87, (1989), pp. 1139, 1508–1526. For a polemical analysis of the coping mechanisms Justices' Brandeis and Frankfurter used to reconcile acknowledging or ignoring their Jewish identity in light of the WASPish Supreme Courts they served on respectively.
24. Warriner, *Handbook of English,* pp. 37, 39; Lewis, *Correct Spelling,* p. 291.
25. Ibid.
26. In a conversation with historian, musicologist, and prolific author, Arthur R. LaBrew, November 5, 1990, LaBrew stated: "that the rendering of Black people in print in the lowercase has negative implications when read." Even more egregious has been the silent complicity of the entire literary community allowing Blacks, the largest minority group in America, to be identified in print in the lowercase. See *Brown v. Board of Education,* 347 U.S. 483, 494 (1954).
27. U.S. Bureau of Census, *Statistical Abstract of the United States,* Population Reports, 1989, Washington, DC, p. 12. The projected population for Black Americans in 1991 will be 12.4%; (hereinafter U.S. Census); "The Biggest Secret of Race Relations: The New White Minority," *Ebony,* April 1989, pp. 84–88.
28. Martin Luther King, *Why We Can't Wait,* Harper & Row, New York, 1964, p. 93.

2
Racial Designations in the Bible

Whenever any group, tribe, race, nation, or their descendants were spoken of in the Bible, it was always in the uppercase. In the seventeenth-century, pro-slavery England, under the reign of King James I, the mandate was given to an elite and erudite group of literary scholars, poets, and theologians to translate the Holy Bible from the original Aramaic, Hebrew, and Greek languages, into the vernacular so that the common people could read and understand God's word for themselves in plain English. All the words which would later refer to "Black people" were put in capital letters as the ancient languages delineated all nations to be cited. James Felder, in his book *Troubling Biblical Waters: Race, Class, and Family,* cites in his introduction R. A. Morrisey's *Colored People and Bible History,* and states the following startling fact, " . . . the biblical genealogies of Genesis 10 and 1 Chronicles 1, affirming that all the descendants of Ham, beginning with Cush, Egypt (Mizraim), Put (Punt) [Phut], and Canaan, were basically Negroes."[1] Cush is the ancient word for Ethiopia. In Genesis 10:6–10, and I Chronicles 1:8–12, the genealogy of what later became known as the *Black* race were cited as: "sons of Ham," "Cush" (=Ethiopia), "Mizraim," "Phut," "Canaan." For example, Genesis 10:6 states that, "And the sons of Ham; Cush, and Mizraim, and Phut, and Canaan," and in I Chronicles 1:8 that, "The sons of Cush; Seba, and Havilah, and Sabath . . . and the sons of Raamah; Sheba and Dedan." There were many great Black patriarchs in the Bible that were descendants of Noah's second son, Ham. For example, the patriarchs: "Seba" and "Sheba," were probably progenitors of the legendary "Queen of Sheba," who came from Ethiopia to personally view for herself the legendary splendors of King Solomon's Court. In I Kings 10:, the writer states, "And when the queen of Sheba heard of the fame of Solomon concerning the name of the Lord, she came to prove him with hard questions." Another person of color from the genealogy of Ham was Nimrod—the first world ruler of the world's first great empire, Babylon (modern Iraq), where the famous "tower of Babel" was built. The account given in Genesis 10:8–10 states, " . . . Cush begat Nimrod . . . he was a mighty hunter . . . Nimrod the mighty hunter before the Lord . . . the beginning of his kingdom was Babel . . . " Abraham's servant and concubine was a *Black* Egyptian named Hagar, who became the mother of the Arab nations. Genesis 16:1 states that, "Now Sarai Abram's wife bare him no children: and she had a handmaid, an Egyptian, whose name was Hagar." Note here that Hagar's racial/national identity [Egyptian] is always capitalized in the Bible.

The New Testament isn't without Black representation, and like the Old Testament, all racial identities are in the uppercase. For example, there were two prominent leaders in the first century Christian Church named Niger and Lucius, their names are found in Acts 13:1, "Now there were in the church that was at Antioch certain prophets and teachers; as Barnabas, and Simeon that was called Niger, and Lucius of Cyrene. . . . " Niger is a country located in sub-Sahara West Africa, Cyrene was a city in North Africa that was heavily populated by Black Africans in the First Century A.D. In this passage there is a strong probability that several of the early church fathers were Black Africans. In Matthew 12:42, and Luke 11:31, Jesus Christ himself states that, "The queen of the South (i.e., Ethiopia) shall rise up in the judgment with the men of this generation." Another queen from Ethiopia named Candace, sent an envoy headed by her chief aide, "the Ethiopian Eunuch," to Jerusalem to worship God during the annual feast days. In Acts 8:26–40, the narrative states, "... the angel of the Lord spake unto Philip... go... unto Gaza... [there you will meet] a man of Ethiopia, an eunuch of great authority under Candace queen of the Ethiopians... [for they] had come to Jerusalem for to worship." Note here that the eunuch's racial identity is capitalized. The irony here is had this passage been written in contemporary America, with all its civil rights and civil liberties laws on the books, that same passage would have probably been written like this: "John, a black man from Africa, came to America to worship God...."

Perhaps law scholars, sociologists, and other academicians should take a lesson from the Bible on how to properly delineate racial groups in print. First of all, the Bible rarely addresses anyone by the color of their skin. That would not only be considered insignificant, but offensive to Eastern mores, and inconsequential to any viable understanding of that person's character or of who that person actually is on an intrinsic level. Secondly, the Bible, when addressing a particular race, generally uses *national,* not *racial* designations. In the Mosaic writings, such national designations as "children of Israel" are noted. For example, in Exodus 1:7: "And the children of Israel were fruitful, and increased abundantly..." and in I Chronicles 1:5: "The sons of Japheth; Gomer, and Magog, and Madai and Javan, and Tubal, and Meshech, and Tiras." This chapter designates the three major genealogical divisions from Noah's three sons, Shem, Ham, and Japheth, who repopulated the earth after the Great Flood. Later on in the Biblical narrative, national designations were shortened by the suffix, "ites" (i.e., Canaanites, Jebusites, Amorites). During the time of King David, nations were identified by the country they were from respectively: For example, Philista (Philistines), Babylon (Baby-

Ionians), Moab (Moabites). In the New Testament, racial identity was always from a nationalist rather than any external, superficial designation as color, "Samaritan," "Ethiopian," "Syro-Phoenician," "Sons of Judah," "Sons of Levi." These are just a few of the many *Black* people found in critical roles throughout the Bible. Thus, the Bible gives significance to all nations of the world equally. Yet American legal scholars, at the dawn of the twenty-first century, still subjugate and segregate 12% of the American population, over 25 million people, to the cursory epithet, *black,* when referring to them in print. The word, *black,* in its lowercase designation, has no more meaning than the abstract color it represents. Perhaps another reason that *black* is preferred is because most people tend to refer to *Black* Americans as, "those people" or "others." For example, Kimberly Crenshaw Williams states that, "Yet they [the critics] fail to acknowledge the limited range of potions presented to *Blacks* in a context where they were deemed *other,*"[2] and " . . . the continuing role of *Black* Americans as *other.*"[3]

In many scholarly works, the racial designation, *black,* is used as an adjective, not *Black,* as a proper noun, as other races are characterized. Even in international discourse, *black* in the lowercase is deemed insignificant and unimportant—a convenient label to identify what many *White* Americans and lately, Japanese leaders consider Black people as an ignorant, mongrel, and indolent race, unworthy of capital designation in print or deserving respect. For example, the then Prime Minister of Japan, Yasuhiro Nakasone, made derogatory remarks concerning *Blacks,* Puerto Ricans, and Mexicans and said, "contending that the average intelligence in the U.S. was lower than Japan because of the minorities."[4] Serioku Kajiyama, Japan's Prime Minister of Justice, remarked that, "It's like in America when neighborhoods become *mixed* because *blacks* move in and *whites are forced* out."[5] Such inflammatory statements as these from respected foreign leaders, does little in eradicating racism and discriminatory practices against America's most vulnerable citizens, who shamefully are labeled daily in the print media by the cursory epitaph *black*.

The whole idea of racial delineation in America is at best plebeian. Historically, race has primarily been determined from the perspective of who had "black blood" in their genealogy. In general, state statutory law pre-1920's stated that a person was considered a *negro* if he had "one-eighth negro blood." This was the so-called *octoroon*. A Louisiana statute law during the same period seemingly contradicted the previous definition stating that, "then one-eighth negro blood is *not* a person of the negro or black race concerning octoroons."[6] Other states like Kentucky, Missouri, and Tennessee—forsaking an arbitrary definition in favor of a genealogical one—considered a person of Negro ancestry if there was in a person's bloodline a "person of negro descent to the third generation inclusive, or the like."[7] A Virginia statute had an even broader definition to be considered a negro—"a person with one-fourth or more of negro blood." This was the so-called *quadroon*.[8]

In a speech given at a Detroit church that I attended during the fall of 1990, Harvard Associate Professor of Psychiatry, Dr. Alvin Poussaint, structured an antithetical paradigm in determining race delineation in America, placing the emphasis on the amount of *White* blood in a person's genealogy as the determining factor in racial identity. Dr. Poussaint's antithetical corollary is paraphrased as follows: What if blackness was the favored norm in America and to be considered legally *Black,* you had to have not more than 1/8th White in you? Of course this view would be considered just as ludicrous as our present day system of racial classification with little scientific, historical, or moral viability. It seems that our present system of racial determination in America is unnecessary, arbitrary and capricious; breeding hostility and balkanization among its racial groups.

Notes

1. R. A. Morrisey, *Colored People and Bible History,* Orbis Books, Maryknoll, NY, 1925, pp. 6–7; cited by James Felder, *Troubling Biblical Waters: Race, Class, and Family,* Orbis Books, Maryknoll, NY, 1989, p. xii. For a more detailed account on Biblical genealogy, see D. L. Willmington, *Willmington's Guide to the Bible,* Tyndale House Publishers, Wheaton, IL, 1981, pp. 12–13.
2. Crenshaw, Kimberly Williams, "Race, Reform and Retrenchment: Transformation and Legitimation in Antidiscrimination Law," *Harvard Law Review,* 101, (1988), p. 1332.
3. Ibid., p. 1385: " . . . the continuing role of Black Americans as *other*" (emphasis mine).
4. "The Crises in Black America," *Detroit News,* September 30, 1990, p. B-5.
5. Ibid.
6. Other states forsaking an arbitrary definition considered a person of Negro ancestry if there was in a person's bloodline a "person of negro descent to the third generation inclusive, or the like." *State v. Treadaway,* 52 So. 500 (La.).
7. Kentucky Statues, 1909, sec. 4615; Missouri Revised. Statutes, 1899 sec 2174; Code of Tennessee, 1896, sec. 4186.
8. Code of Virginia, 1873, c. 103, sec. 2; *Jones v. Commonwealth,* 80 Va. 538; *Harvard Law Review,* 24, (1910–11), pp. 68–9.

3
Arguments Against Racial Capitalization Addressed and Refuted

1. "black" has always been written in the lowercase in all forms of print

Invariably, there will be those who are reading this essay who will have one of several arguments *against* capitalizing the word *Black* when addressing African Americans in print. The first argument—*tradition, states that the racial designation, Black, has always been written in the lowercase in all forms of print. It is not meant to be derogatory or of secondary significance, so let's just leave it like it is.* Many traditions are good and help society maintain strong cultural ties and solidifies shared values. However, traditions are not *ipso facto* sacrosanct. For example, it was Christ who broke with tradition when he healed the lunatic, deaf, blind, lame, and mute on the Jewish Holy Day—the Sabbath. This was the one day of the week, according to the law of Moses, that no work was to be done. When Jesus was confronted by the Jewish religious leaders about breaking the law of Moses by healing the infirm on the Sabbath, He asked the following series of rhetorical questions: "Is it better to heal on the Sabbath?" "Which of you shall have an ass or an ox fallen into a pit, and will not straightway pull him out on the Sabbath?" Concluding with: "The Sabbath was made for man and not man for the Sabbath."[1] In Western philosophy, Socrates broke with tradition, criticizing the Greek city–states as corrupt, immoral, and mercenary. History records that, "He was accused of impropriety and innovation and was forced to commit suicide by drinking hemlock."[2] In music, Johann Sebastian Bach (1685–1750), that preeminent classical composer, organist, violinist, *Kapellmeister* (Choir director) of the baroque period, refused to compose in the most popular musical form of his day—Opera, because of its frivolity, excesses, and lack of gravity and spirituality, but instead wrote primarily sacred music often signing his work with the epigram, SDG (*Soli Dei Gloria*= To God alone be the Glory). Bach created no musical forms himself, but developed, summarized, and brought to their climax of perfection, the existing musical forms of his day to such an extent as to forever change the course of Western Art music.[3] So tradition, although good for codifying shared cultural values and defining morals, is never right to use tradition in defense of bigotry, prejudice, and racially discriminatory policies, such as using the lower case when referring to certain racial groups in print.

2. Leave Black in the lowercase, because white isn't capitalized

This argument limits the terms *Black/White* to mere colors and ignores their historical use as racial descriptions. When using these words to delineate race, you are describing much more than an abstract color, but an entire culture, heritage, experience, identity, and existence.[4] Not only should the words *Black* and *White* be capitalized in print when discussing race, but allow me to add the *caveat* that it is inherently more expedient for the legal community to capitalize *Black* as opposed to *White,* for when people read about *Black* people in print, rarely is it of good report. It usually concerns some egregious act such as homicide, drugs, aggravated battery, robbery, incarceration, child abuse, divorce or an endless litany of negative statistics about why *Black* people generally have a shorter life expectancy, are less intelligent than other racial groups, etc. When the average person reads only about *Black* pathology and aberrant behavior day in and day out, by a society which already views *Black* people as an ignorant, criminal, promiscuous, inferior, marginal, and a segregated race, it is quite easy then for the reader to reach the conclusion that not only is the *Black* race inferior to all other races, but that its inferiority is pathological, genetic, and immutable. However, when a reader sees the word *white* in the lowercase, no such anomalies are attributed, for *White* Americans have their built-in *success factors* to combat any and every aberration from members of its ranks. For example, if one reads a newspaper article or watches a TV program about a young *White* girl with several children born out of wedlock by several different fathers, on public assistance, on drugs, with little hope for a viable future, the general [White] viewer will project that this poor maiden is certainly the exception and not the rule in her race, and usually will not generalize or stereotype aberrant behavior of one or a subgroup onto the entire *White* race. Also, for every poor, unproductive or otherwise dysfunctional *White* person in America, there will be hundreds or even thousands of CEOs, doctors, lawyers, or otherwise highly trained, skilled, and consistently productive *White* Americans to combat the aberrant behavior of that one *White* person who is merely viewed as an exception to the rule. The lowercase designation of *black* also underscores the secondary status *Black* Americans have always been segregated to in America, which the lowercase designation of *white* will never have in light of their primary status level in America and throughout the world. In other words, people don't accord secondary or diminutive status to *White* people when they see the spelling—*white, but this lowercase designation becomes exceedingly more acute when used in relation to Black* Americans identified as *black.* To the *White* person, it is one more affirmation of their privileged position and a subtle but potent belief in the second-class status of the Black race. It is like one more unnecessary hindrance in the *Black* American's quest for "equal justice under the law." This is because *Black* Americans, as citizens, are considered secondary, inferior, and, in general, less intelligent than other racial groups in America. Thus, *White* American's superiority is preserved, its status unfettered by lowercase designation in print. However, in the interest of fairness and consistency, I believe that the racial designation, *White,* should still be capitalized whenever it addresses an individual or a group by race for the very same reasons I have outlined above.

3. Black is a synonym for the term minority

This argument ignores the fact that the latter term *minority* is an adjective used exclusively for descriptive purposes. For example: *The political party many minorities support has been traditionally Democratic.* Here minorities represent not a specific group or race as the term *Black* does, but a group of races (i.e., Blacks, Hispanics, Native Americans, and Asians). Since no one particular race is delineated with the term "minority," then proper rules of grammar dictate that you may use a lowercase "m" unless when used in a title[5] or at the beginning of a sentence.[6] Ebony magazine,[7] one of the few publications on the market to consistently use the uppercase when referring to the *Black* race, recently ran an article on the trend in current literature to use the term *African American* instead of *black* to describe *Black* people. As mentioned at the beginning of the Essay, using the word African, to delineate *Black* people in

America isn't without precedent. *Black* Americans historically utilized the term African in many of the titles and writings associated with their churches, music, theater, and intellectual organizations prior to 1900.[8] For example, historian and musicologist A. R. LaBrew, in his book, *Black Music and Musical Taste in New York City* (1800–1850) cites that the first all-Black Christian Church in America was founded in Philadelphia by Bishop Richard Allen in the early nineteenth century and was called—the *African Methodist Episcopal Church* (A.M.E.). Other Black churches of the period were called: *African Church, African Episcopal, African Free, and African Methodist Episcopal Zion. The African Society, and the New York African Society for Mutual Relief* were both *Black* philanthropic organizations. In 1821, the *African Grove Theater* was founded by middle and upper class *Black* people in New York as a forum for secular theater which was beginning to flourish. The *African Grecian Ball* was an annual social event founded by the *African Grecian Society* in New York. This intellectual society was started in 1827 by Black people in New York and its surrounding areas. One of the pictures I've seen in Mr. LaBrew's personal collection shows one of these balls being attended by the Governor of New York. These free *Black* Americans sought to align themselves to the Greek ideals of freedom, liberty and equality for all mankind, and at the same time actively sought freedom for their brothers held in the bonds of chattel slavery in the South.

In scholarly legal publications like law reviews and law journals, the only references that I was able to find that capitalizes the word *Black* when directly relating to an individual or racial group was in the *Howard University Law Journal*. Howard University is a historically Black university in Washington, D.C., established during the Reconstruction period to educate newly freed former slaves from the South and *Blacks* from the North who wanted to pursue a college education. For example, Justice Clarence Thomas, then Chairman of the EEOC (Equal Employment Opportunity Commission), wrote in the *Howard University Law Journal,* "The Bicentennial of the Constitution challenges all Americans but must strike *Black* Americans with particular poignancy. . . . In order to include *Black* Americans in the Constitution. . . . "[9]

4. Since Black and White are adjectives, they shouldn't be spelled using the uppercase.

It is true that most adjectives, even those describing personal pronouns, receive lowercase designation. However, the racial designations, *Black* and *White,* are also nouns when describing racial or national origins (i.e., Italian, Jewish, German, African) becomes (Italian American, Jewish American, etc. . . .), the capital designation is grammatically correct. An excerpt from *The World Book Dictionary* entry for the racial term, *Black,* should shed more light on the issue:

> black (adj.) . . . 7 b. Also Black. Negro . . . n. 3 b. Also, Black, a Negro. White (adj.) 5 a. having a light-colored skin, not black, brown, red, or yellow. Caucasian . . . n. 6. a white person; person of the Caucasian race. . . . 10. Often, White.[10]

The Reader's Digest Encyclopedia Dictionary entry for *Black* and *White* reads as follows:

> Black 4. Having a very dark skin, as a Negro . . . n. 3. A member of the so-called black race; a Negro. White, 14. Of, pertaining to, or governed by the white race: white supremacy.[11]

The footnote at the bottom of the page of *The World Book Dictionary* lists some interesting historical background information regarding the racial designation, *Black*. I have italicized all racial designations for emphasis:

> *Black,* meaning *Negro,* was formerly seldom used in American English in formal writing and speech except when referring contemptuously to *Negroes.* In the mid–1960's, however, *black* began to gain currency, but this time on a respectable level, as ethnic groups promoted labels with such slogans as "*Black* is Beautiful." Now *black* is widely used in referring to the ethnic group and its enterprises and organizations (*black* capitalism, *black* power, *Black* Muslims), but is still considered in some quarters, particularly among older *Negroes* and *whites,* as somewhat contemptuous.[12]

What these excerpts from various well-known American dictionaries shows us is that even our language's most trusted and used repository for proper grammar, vocabulary, and word meaning, are inconsistent in whether to use upper or lower-case designation when referring to *Black* people. Apparently, lexicographers are either unconcerned or unsure concerning proper designation of *Black/White* when addressing racial groups to make a definitive entry. The following example further shows how inconsistent most American dictionaries are in the use of proper racial delineation in print: "*white* backlash, a hostile reaction on the part of whites to *Negro* demands for racial equality."[13] In this sentence, the word *Negro* is capitalized and the word, *White* isn't. The inconsistency among lexicographers in racial designation in print needs much improvement.

"black" or "Black:" Separate, but Equal

Concerning aspects of Constitutional law, namely, the Thirteenth, Fourteenth, and Fifteenth Amendments, are a triumvirate of Supreme Court decisions that are indispensable in discussing issues of segregation. Namely, *Dred Scott v. Sandford*[14] *Plessey v. Ferguson,*[15] and *Brown v. Board of Education.*[16] If one would draw a continuum, showing the interrelatedness of these three seminal civil rights cases, and the ground work each case laid for the next, it would look something like this:

YEAR	CASE	HOLDING
1875	Dred Scott v. Sandford	"[Negroes are] altogether unfit to associate with the white race...."
1896	Plessey v. Ferguson	"separate, but equal...."
1954	Brown v. Board of Education	"separate is inherently unequal."
1978	California v. Bakke	"No person . . . shall be excluded from participation in any program receiving federal assistance."[17]

Another reason to use the uppercase when writing about racial groups is found in both the *Plessey* and *Brown* cases. Each case invoked scientific data to show that there is a provable correlation of lowering self-esteem and separate facilities or educational opportunities. For example, Charles Lofgren, in a book on the *Plessey* case, wrote: "Whatever may have been the extent of psychological knowledge at the time of *Plessey v. Ferguson,* this finding (used to prove that separate schools are inherently inferior, thus creating or acerbating feelings of inferiority with black school children) is amply supported by modern authority."[18] How much more would the separate and inferior racial designation (black) contribute to "creating" or acerbating feelings of inferiority," not only with *Black* school children, but with an entire racial group.

How *Black* Americans have described themselves, or have been described, has been through many developments. For example, the term *Negro* was first used by early Spanish and Portuguese explorers to identify the African slaves which they took to the New World in 1501.[19] According to *The Compact Edition of the Oxford English Dictionary*, the word, *Negro*, first appeared in English print in 1555: "They are not accustomed to eat such meats as do the Ethiopians or Negroes."[20] As slaves in America, usage of our language, names, or customs were strictly forbidden. *Black* people were usually given names by their masters. (My father, Ivan Washington, told me that this was how our forefathers received the Washington surname). After Emancipation, many *Blacks* made up last names, kept the name of their previous master, or adopted names that they saw or heard before that suited them. From the colonial period through the 1950's, some of the generic designations African Americans were referred to were: *nigger, mulatto, quadroon, octoroon, colored, negro,* or *New Negro.* "New Negro" was a term coined by Marcus Garvey's Universal Negro Improvement Association (UNIA) in the early 1920's.[21] During the socially turbulent 1950's and 60's, *Black* consciousness was raised to an unprecedented level, culminating in several pivotal civil rights desegregation cases, *Brown v. Board of Education,*[22] being the most famous, and ending with three federal acts, signed into law by President Lyndon Johnson: namely the Voting Rights Act of 1965[23] and the Civil Rights Acts of 1964[24] and the Civil Rights Act of 1968.[25] During this period, *"Black"* was the preferred term used by African American's to reaffirm their identity. James Brown, the soul music star in the late 1960's, wrote a song extolling *Black* Americans new found pride in their color: "Say it loud, I'm *Black* and I'm proud." By the 1960's the term *Afro-American* was more frequently found in print.[26]

So offensive was the term *black,* some older African Americans have stated that before the 1950's, if you called a *Negro* person *Black*, you were asking for a fight. Partly because of racism and segregation in America, the word *Black* had become such a scurrilous and reactionary term that it had become synonymous with a curse word, or had became just as offensive as calling a *Black* person a *Nigger.* In retrospect, this is as ironic as it is ludicrous, for as mentioned earlier, the term *Negro* is simply the Spanish word for dark, or *black.* Now here we are in the 1990's and the term *black* is used almost exclusively in legal scholarship as well as in many of our leading newspapers, periodicals, and magazines when referring to *Black* people. For example, the following excerpts show how some of America's most widely read newspapers and news magazines delineate racial groups in print. I have italicized all racial designations for emphasis:

- *The New York Times* on race states that, "Dr. Robert Hayles, a *black* psychologist . . . at *Swedish* meatballs. . . . "

These quotes are particularly interesting because the word *Black,* in "black psychologist" and *Swedish,* in "Swedish meatballs," are both used as descriptive adjectives. Swedish meatballs is capitalized, however, black psychologist, which has much more significance being a highly trained scholar possessing the highest degree in academia, is reflected in print as secondary to an inanimate object—a meatball! Other examples of lowercase designation of its racial groups are evident throughout the article:

- "I've been at parties where *whites* have asked how *black* people feel about Jesse Jackson."[27]
- *The Detroit News*—"President George Bush brushing aside appeals from civil rights groups and advice from key *black* Republicans . . . "[28]
- *The Chicago Tribune*—"Jesse Jackson's organization, Operation P.U.S.H., initiated a . . . boycott . . . against Nike . . . claiming that they were disrespectful to *blacks* . . . "[29]
- *The Los Angeles Times*—"they set through harangues

- against dropping out in which their teacher cites role models such as *black* economist Thomas Sowell."[30]
- *Time*—"As Mahalia Jackson chimed in, King concluded with the resounding hope that *blacks* and *whites* would join hands to sing, in the words of an old *Negro* spiritual,"[31] and "The success of the civil rights movement contributed to the continuance of the *Underclass*. The removal of many racial barriers allowed *blacks* who had made it to get out of the ghetto."[32]

Note that the racial aberration, *Underclass,* is capitalized, but *black,* isn't. It seems like the media is emphasizing the negative labels given to *Black* people rather than citing who *Black* people really are as human beings. Don't *Blacks* amount to more than being the *Underclass*?

- *U.S. News and World Report*—"Since at least 1900, American *blacks* have accounted for a disproportionate share of murder victims and perpetrators."[33]
- *Newsweek*—"Nowhere is this more true than in the increasingly acrimonious relations between *blacks* and *Hispanics.*"[34]
- *The Nation* magazine—"Two-thirds would be *black,* one-quarter *white* and the rest *Latino* and *Asian,* making it the most ethnically diverse city in Massachusetts."[35]
- *The New Republic*—"Today's *black* Americans are the beneficiaries of great historical achievements."[36]

There is a movement now in the literary community to change from calling *Black* Americans *Black* to *African American*. The former term emphasizing an arbitrary skin pigmentation. The latter affirming a person's racial, ethnic, cultural, and historic identity as well as their present national citizenship as Americans.[37] Sometimes, the quandary whether to delineate *Black* Americans as—*Black* or *black,* can be solved by creative thinking—use both spellings. For example, in the book review by Julius Chambers, he wrote, "the dramatic increase in the number of *black* elected officials across the country is one notable example. Yet despite these advances, *Blacks* still hold fewer than 1.5 percent of elective offices in the United States . . . "[38] In feminist literature, racial delineation is also inconsistent. For example, in Russo's book review on Angela Davis's book, *Women, Race and Class,* she wrote, "According to [Angela] Davis, *Black* women's oppression . . . ." However, earlier in the same volume, in an article by McKay, the lowercase "b" is used in the opening sentence "The history of *black* people in America . . . " Even in anti-racist literature such as Bettmann's, *Anti-Klan Newsletter,* published by the Partisan Defense Committee, the lowercase *b* is used. Bettmann writes: "Today as *black* America is under the gun. . . . The history of *black* people in America."[39]

In books by *Black* writers, or in *Black* owned publications, racial capitalization is generally (but not always) more consistent, however, the dilemma of whether to use *black* or *Black* is still there. For example, some *Black* scholars and writers utilize *black/white* as their racial designations. Among those scholars are, psychiatrist and Afrocentrist, Dr. Frances Cress Welsing, in her book, *The Cress Theory of Color- Confrontation and Racism (White Supremacy)*; Nathan Fuller, *Textbook for Victims of White Supremacy*;[40] Julius Chambers, book review of M. Belknap, *Federal Law and Southern Order: Racial Violence and Constitutional Conflict in the Post Brown South,* used both racial designations and stated, "the dramatic increase in the number of *black* elected officials across the country is one notable example. Yet despite these advances, *Blacks* still hold fewer than 1.5 percent of elective offices in the United States. . . . "[41] The 1988 U.S. Census shows that, "The average life expectancy at birth for *whites* is 5.8 years longer than for *Blacks*."[42] *The Brown case* used *Negro/white* throughout its opinion: "Segregation of *white* and *Negro* children in the public schools. . . . "[43] This is not only inconsistent, but is just as unfair as when *White* authors use the dichotomy, *Black/white,* or *Negro/white,* in print.[44] In *The Black Collegian,* journalist and TV host Tony Brown wrote, "The *Black* community is in a seriously deteriorating condition."[45] *The Michigan Chronicle,* "The late Adam Clayton Powell was one of many noted *Black* political officials . . . "[46] all utilize the uppercase when referring to *Black* Americans. *Black* publications didn't always use the uppercase when referring to *Black* Americans. For example, *Ebony* magazine in a 1977 article wrote, "Like those millions of *blacks*, uprooted from Mother Africa and enslaved on foreign shores."[47] *The Crisis,* an NAACP organ, still utilizes the lowercase "b" when referring to *Black* Americans stated, "Over a century and a half passed between the arrival of the first *blacks* in America in 1619."[48]

Is it possible that this literary omission could be a cause of why *Black* Americans are at the bottom of most positive statistics (i.e., IQ or aptitude tests) and are at the top of most negative statistics? For example, studies have shown that the decline in the African American socio-economic position has been paralleled by an increase in overt acts of racial hostility toward them. In a noted article on racial bias in testing by Howard and Hammond, wrote, "[T]he difference between the combined median scores of *blacks* and *whites* on the verbal and math portions of the SAT was slightly more than 200 points . . . in recent years less than half of all *black* students have achieved a combined score of 700 on the SAT."[49] Might some of this negativism be lessened if *Black* Americans were positively identified in print with capital designation? True, this might be a stretch, but it isn't beyond the realm of reality. For example, Chambers notes that, "The gap between *African Americans* and *Whites* in practically every socio-economic category has widened in the last twenty years."[50] Williams states that, the African American poverty rate in 1986 was 31%, it was 11% for *Whites,* and that "*Black* median income is 57 percent that of *whites,* a decline of about four percentage points since the early 1970's. Average annual family income for African Americans dropped 9% from the 1970's to the 1980's."[51] The study by Lauter and May further notes that since 1969, the proportion of *Black* men between 25 and 55 earning less than $5,000 a year rose from 8% to 20%. Williams notes that African American enrollment in universities and colleges is also on the decline, and that, "The average life expectancy at birth for whites is 5.8 years longer than for *Blacks.* According to the *U.S. Bureau of Census, Statistical Abstract of the United States,* in 1986 the life expectancy at birth of *white* females was 78.9 years; of *black* females, 73.6; of *white* males, 72.0; and *black* males 65.5."[52]

Conclusion

Could racial discrimination towards African Americans in print be alleviated or lessened by capitalizing something as seemingly insignificant as the word *"black"* when used as a racial designation in print? Could giving the most brutalized and maligned people in American history a jot or tittle of dignity, legitimization, and significance in print somehow raise African Americans perceptual viability? To other racial groups? To themselves? It is my contention that Black Americans' negative self-perception, and perhaps other racial groups' negative perception of them, could be lessened, at least to some small degree, if all references to race in print would use the uppercase "B" when writing about *Black* people.[53] To rectify this inequity, I have outlined that the following proposals should be implemented: (1) All law reviews, journals, judicial opinions, and legal publications including reporters, digests, and lexicons, in America should adopt the uppercase designation when referring to *Black* people in print as officially codified in the manual: *A Uniform System for Citation* as followed in the *Howard University Law Review;*[54] That legal scholars challenge the continued use of lowercase *"b"* in all forms of print starting at the Federal level (i.e., U. S. Bureau of Census and the U.S. Commission of Civil Rights), and continuing through the state and local levels of government; (3) All daily newspapers and national magazines (i.e., the *New York Times, Boston Globe, Washington Post, Los Angeles Times, Time, Newsweek, U.S. News and World Report,* the *New Yorker, Harpers, The New Republic, National Review,* the *Weekly Standard,* the *Social Critic,* etc. . . .), should use the upper case when referring to racial groups or individuals; (4) All books, treatises, encyclopedias, dictionaries, and any other form of print media should follow the recommendations outlined above. Then and only then can legal scholarship (and eventually all forms of serious writing) be truly devoted to subjugating discrimination in print, for as Shakespeare said, "the pen is mightier than the sword."

Notes

1. Luke 14:3; Mark 2:27.
2. *Reader's Digest Dictionary,* p. 1273.
3. See generally, Hans T. David and Arthur Mendel, eds., *The Bach Reader,* W. W. Norton & Co., New York, 1966.
4. Katherine Mackinnon, "Feminism Marxism, Method and the State: An Agenda for Theory, 7 Signs," *Journal of Women in Culture & Society,* pp. 515–16 (1982).
5. *A Uniform System of Citation,* Cambridge, MA, 1986, pp. 31, 84, 91, hereinafter *Manual;* John E. Warriner, *Handbook of English,* Harcourt, Brace & World, Inc., NY, 1948, pp. 37, 39, Norman Lewis, *Correct Spelling Made Easy,* Dell Publishing Co., NY, 1963, p. 291.

6. *Manual,* pp. 31, 84, 91; for example, as in the title: Harold Cruse, *Plural but Equal: Blacks and Minorities in America's Plural Society,* William Morrow, New York, 1987.
7. "African-American or Black: What's in a Name?" *Ebony,* July 1989, pp. 79–80.
8. In discussing the matter of whether or not the word, *Black* should be capitalized in print with a historian and friend Arthur R. La Brew, he stated that, "the rendering of Black people in print in the lowercase has negative implications when read." Arthur R. LaBrew, *Black Music and Musical Taste in New York City*(1800–1850), Michigan Music Research Center, Detroit, 1983, pp. 5, 30, 44: The first Black Christian denomination was started by Bishop Allen in the early 19th century and was called *African Methodist Episcopal Church* (A.M.E.), other Black churches of the period were called: *African Church, African Episcopal, African Free,* and *African Methodist Episcopal Zion. The African Society, and the New York African Society for Mutual Relief* were both Black philanthropic organizations. By 1821, the *African Grove Theater* was founded by New York Blacks as a forum for secular theater which was beginning to flourish. The *African Grecian Ball* was an annual social event started by the African Grecian Society in New York. This intellectual society was started in 1827 by New York area Blacks. These free Black Americans sought to align themselves to the Greek ideals of libertarianism and egalitarianism for all mankind.
9. Clarence Thomas, "Toward A Plain Reading of the Constitution—the Declaration of Independence in Constitutional Interpretation," *Howard Law Journal,* 30, (1987), p. 983.
10. *The World Book Dictionary,* Field Enterprises Education Corp., Chicago, 1969, p. 207.
11. *Reader's Digest Dictionary,* p. 1531.
12. *World Book Dictionary,* p. 2385.
13. Ibid.
14. *Dred Scott v. Sandford,* 60 U.S. 393 (1875).
15. *Plessey v. Ferguson,* 163 U.S. 537 (1896).
16. *Brown v. Board of Education,* 347 U.S. 483 (1954).
17. A *Regents of the University of California v. Bakke,* 438 U.S. 265 (1978). The Court held that Title VI of the Civil Rights Act of 1965 must be held to proscribe only those racial classifications that would violate the Equal Protection Clause of the fifth amendment.
18. See Book Note, *Michigan Law Review,* 87, (1989), pp. 1157-1165, reviewing Charles A. Lofgren, "The Plessey Case: A Legal-Historical Interpretation." How much more would a separate and inferior racial designation (black) contribute to "creating" and acerbating "feelings

of inferiority," not only with Black school children, but with an entire racial group.
19. W. Bridgwater and S. Kurtz, eds., *The Illustrated Columbia Encyclopedia*, Columbia University Press, New York, 1963, p. 435.
20. *Negro* first appeared in English print in 1555. Eden Decades, 239: "They are not accustomed to eat such meats as do the Ethiopians or Negroes." Cited by *The Compact Edition of The Oxford English Dictionary*, Oxford University Press, New York, 1981, p. 1910.
21. See generally, Tony Martin, *Race First: The Ideological and Organizational Struggles of Marcus Garvey and The Universal Negro Improvement Association*, 1976; J. A. Rogers, *World's Great Men of Color*, 1947; E. Frazier, *Black Bourgeoisie,* Collier-Macmillan, New York, 1962.
22. *Brown v. Board of Education*, 347 U.S. 483 (1954).
23. Voting Rights Act of 1965.
24. Civil Rights Act of 1964. 18 U.S.C. sec. 241, (1964), making illegal any acts which deprive citizens their rights; 18 U.S.C. sec. 242, (1964), making illegal violators of deprivation of rights under color of law.
25. Civil Rights Act of 1968. Pub. L. No. 90-284, Title I, sec. 101(a), 82 Stat. 73, (1968) (codified as amended at 18 U.S.C., sec. 245), criminal statute that prohibited deprivation of anyone's right to vote or to participate in any activities concerning the United States government.
26. *African-American or Black?," pp. 78–80.*
27. Williams, "Uneasy Mingling: When Small Talk at Parties Tackles Large Racial Issues," *New York Times,* October 21, 1988, p. A-15, col. 1: "Dr. Robert Hayles, a *black psychologist at . . . Swedish meatballs . . .* ") *(emphasis added)*. "I've been at parties where *whites* have asked how *black* people feel about Jesse Jackson") *(emphasis mine).*
28. Moore, "Bush Ignores Pleas, Vetoes Rights Bill," *Detroit News-Free Press,* October 23, 1990, p. 1-A, col. 5: "President George Bush, brushing aside appeals from civil rights groups and advice from key *black* Republicans . . . " *(emphasis mine).*
29. See generally, Mike Royko, "No, Nike's. Still Not Shaking in Its Boots," *Chicago Tribune,* October 2, 1990, Sec. 1, p. 3.
30. Hamilton, "A Matter of Style, Math Teacher's Methods Draw Praise and a Probe," *Los Angeles Times,* November 27, 1990, Sec. B, col. B: ". . . they set through harangues against dropping out in which their teacher cites role models such as *black* economist Thomas Sowell" (emphasis mine).
31. Sheppard, "A Time for Heroes, Not Saints," book review, *Time,* November 28, 1988, p. 95: "As Mahalia Jackson chimed in, King con-

cluded with the resounding hope that *blacks* and *whites* would join hands to sing, in the words of an old Negro spiritual" (emphasis mine).

32. Stengel, "The Underclass: Breaking the Cycle," *Time,* October 10, 1988, p. 41: "The success of the civil rights movement contributed to the continuance of the Underclass. The removal of many racial barriers allowed *blacks* who had made it to get out of the ghetto" *(emphasis added).*

33. Moore, "The Black-On-Black Crime Plague," *U.S. News and World Report,* August 22, 1988, p. 48: "Since at least 1900, American *blacks* have accounted for a disproportionate share of murder victims and perpetrators." *(emphasis added).*

34. Salholz, "A Conflict of the Have-Nots," *Newsweek,* December 12, 1988, p. 28: "Nowhere is this more true than in the increasingly acrimonious relations between *blacks* and *Hispanics*" *(emphasis added).*

35. House, "Blacks in Boston Seek to Secede," *The Nation,* November 7, 1988, p. 452: "Two-thirds would be *black,* one-quarter *white* and the rest *Latino* and *Asian,* making it the most ethnically diverse city in Massachusetts. *(emphasis added).*

36. Howard and Hammond, "Rumors of Inferiority," *The New Republic,* September 9, 1985, p. 17: "Today's *black* Americans are the beneficiaries of great historical achievements." *(emphasis added).* MacKinnon, *Feminism,* p. 515–16.

37. See generally, Ulrich Philips, *American Negro Slavery,* D. Appleton and Co., New York, 1918, S. Elkins, *Slavery: A Problem in American Institutional and Intellectual Life,* Massachusetts Institute of Technology Press, Cambridge, 1959; Patrick Moynihan, *The Negro Family: The Case For National Action,* in L. Rainwater & W. Yancey, Eds., *The Moynihan Report and the Politics of Controversy,* Massachusetts Institute of Technology Press, Cambridge, 1967; R. Fogel and S. Engerman, *Time on the Cross: The Economics of American Negro Slavery,* Little Brown, Boston, 1974; Eugene Genovese, *Roll, Jordan, Roll: The World The Slaves Made,* Pantheon Books, New York, 1972; Herbert Gutman, *The Black Family in Slavery and Freedom,* 1750–1925, Pantheon Books, New York, 1976; Bell Hooks, *Talking Back: Thinking Feminist, Thinking Black,* South End Press, Boston, *1989; MacKinnon, "Feminism," pp. 515–516.*

38. Chambers, *Book Review,* p. 1613.

39. Russo, *Women, Race and Class,* book review, Women's Studies International Forum, Vol. 6, No. 2, 1983, p. 249; McKay, "Black Woman Professor–White University," Ibid., p. 143; Bettmann, "All Out to Stop the Ku Klux Klan on Nov. 5!" Partisan Defense Committee Newsletter, October 1988, p. 143.

40. Some authors utilize *"Black"* and *"white"* as their racial designations. See Frances Cress Welsing, *The Cress Theory of Color–Confrontation and Racism (White Supremacy)*, Third World Press, Chicago, 1969, pp. 5, 7–8; See generally, Nathan Fuller, *Textbook for Victims of White Supremacy*, Third World Press, Chicago, 1969.
41. Chambers, (Book Review), *Michigan Law Review*, 87, 1987, p. 1613, reviewing M. Belknap, *Federal Law and Southern Order: Racial Violence and Constitutional Conflict in the Post Brown South*, (1989).
42. U.S. Bureau of Census, Washington, DC, 1988, p. 70: "The average life expectancy at birth for whites is 5.8 years longer than for *Blacks*" (*emphasis mine*).
43. See generally, *Brown v. Board of Education*, 347 U.S. 483 (1954). This is not only inconsistent, but just as unfair as when White authors use the dichotomy *Black/white* or *Negro/white* in print.
44. Harry Edwards, "The Single-Minded Pursuit of Sports, Fame and Fortune is Today Approaching an Institutionalized Triple Tragedy in Black Society," *Ebony*, August, 1988, p. 140.
45. Tony Brown, "Buy Freedom Month," *The Black Collegian*, September/October, 1985, p. 72.
46. McTyre, "Black Leaders Targeted by FBI, Media," *Michigan Chronicle*, September 19–25, 1990, p. I-A, col. 5.
47. Poinsett, *Festac '77*, *Ebony*, May, 1977, p. 33.
48. Jones, "The Black Churches in Historical Perspectives," *The Crisis*, November, 1982, Vol, 89, No. 9, p. 6: "Over a century and a half passed between the arrival of the first *blacks* in America in 1619" (*emphasis mine*).
49. Howard and Hammond, "Rumors," p. 18.
50. Chambers, Book Review, p. 1619.
51. Williams, "Urban League Says Blacks Suffered Loss over Decade," *New York Times*, January 15, 1988, p. A-10, col. I; Williams, p. A-10, col. I.
52. Williams, p. A-10, col. 2; U.S. Bureau of Census, p. 70.
53. See generally, U.S. Commission on Rights, Intimidation and Violence: Racial and Religious Bigotry in America, Washington, DC, 1983, p. 53: 347 U.S. at 494 (*footnote omitted*); cited by Richard Kluger, *Simple Justice*, Knopf, New York, 1975, pp. 705–06.
54. *Manual*, pp. 31–33.

4
Liberal Law and the Scientific Mythology of Evolution: McLean v. Arkansas Board of Education

June 12, 1991

> *Evolution is thus not only anti-Biblical and anti-Christian, but it is utterly unscientific and impossible as well. Evolution has served effectively as the pseudo-scientific basis of atheism, agnosticism, socialism, fascism, and numerous other false and dangerous philosophies over the past centuries.*
> —Henry H. Morris and Marlyn E. Clark

A long-standing and inevitable outgrowth of liberalism's bogus constitutional doctrine of the separation of church and state found root in a little-known federal case in Arkansas in the early 1980s, *McLean v. Arkansas Board of Education*[1]. On one level this case was not that unique because liberals, knowing that their philosophy of radical egalitarianism is sophistic, intellectually untenable, and irrational, must bypass Constitutionalism, the democratic process, the will of "We the People," and resort to using a carefully crafted judicial oligarchy to force its unconstitutional ends on the majority.

The creation–evolution debate dates back to the famous Scopes Monkey Trial of 1925,[2] where the Supreme Court ruled a Tennessee statute unconstitutional that prevented evolution being taught as part of the public school curriculum because it contradicted the creation science account of the origins of creation. Prior to the Scopes Monkey Trial, creation science was the only academic explanation of the origins of mankind. Fifty-seven years later, in *McLean v. Arkansas Board of Education,* the Court ruled unconstitutional the "balanced treatment" approach of teaching creation science with evolution science. The Arkansas judge held that creation science was not science because it was based on the creation account of the origin of mankind as found in the Bible.[3] However, the judge throughout his *McLean* opinion stressed the courts' neutrality on the issue of church and state relations,[4] but, as we shall later see, the McLean court was everything but neutral in its high-handed judicial activist approach against the creation science position. The irony here is irresistible. In less than sixty years, we went from a court ruling that held unconstitutional a state statute prohibiting evolution being taught in the public schools even though creation science had been taught in the public schools for over one hundred years. Presently, creation science cannot be taught in the public schools because the courts (and the liberal judges that preside over them) consider that body of knowledge purely religious and of little scientific value. Thanks to liberal activist judges at all levels of our judicial system and a Supreme Court, the majority of whose members shows little regard for the original understanding of the Constitution, evolution dogma now maintains a total monopoly on intellectual thought in American public schools and universities as an explanation of the scientific origins of creation.

Below are relevant excerpts from Section 4 of Act 590 of the "balanced treatment" statute that the McLean court ruled unconstitutional. The act provides definitions. As used in this Act:

A. "Creation science" means the scientific evidences for

creation and inferences from those scientific evidences. Creation science includes the scientific evidences and related inferences that indicate:
   (1) sudden creation of the universe, energy, and life from nothing;
   (2) the insufficiency of mutation and natural selection in bringing about development of all living kinds from a single organism;
   (3) changes only within fixed limits of originally created kinds of plants and animals;
   (4) separate ancestry for man and apes;
   (5) explanation of the earth's geology by catastrophism, including the occurrence of a worldwide flood; and
   (6) a relatively recent inception of the earth and living kinds.
B. "Evolution science" means the scientific evidences for evolution and inferences from those scientific evidences. Evolution science includes the scientific sciences and related inferences that indicate:
   (1) emergence by naturalistic processes of the universe from disordered matter and emergence of life from nonlife;
   (2) the sufficiency of mutation and natural selection in bringing about development of present living kinds from simple earlier kinds;
   (3) emergence by mutation and natural selection of present living kinds from simple earlier kinds;
   (4) emergence of man from a common ancestor with apes;
   (5) explanation of the earth's geology and the evolutionary sequence by uniformitarianism; and
   (6) an inception several billion years ago of the earth and somewhat later of life.

Public school "means public secondary and elementary schools."
C. Definition of science:
   (1) it is guided by natural law;
   (2) it has to be explanatory by reference to natural law;
   (3) it is testable against the empirical world;
   (4) its conclusions are tentative, i.e., are not necessarily the final word; and
   (5) it is falsifiable.

A major point of constitutional law that was discussed in the plaintiff's argument against the teaching of creation science in the Arkansas public schools was that "[c]ourts are not bound by legislative statements of purpose or legislative disclaimers in determining legislative purpose of statute." This type of rhetoric is classic liberal judicial activism, whereby the judge, in reaching his decision on a case, cares very little about what previous courts or lawmakers have stated on the issue at hand. The only thing that matters to an activist judge is how he "feels" a case should be ruled upon in *this* instance alone and to couch such a decision in pseudo-constitutional language to give his holding the imprimatur of law. The court proceedings in *McLean* serve as a case study of how future case law of this type would be conducted in the matter of teaching creation science along with evolution as a theory of origins in the public schools. On appeal, plaintiff attorneys for McLean (represented by the American Civil Liberties Union, or ACLU) incessantly stigmatized and associated creation science in a pejorative context using buzz words and phrases such as "religion," "God," "The Bible," "nonscientific," and "unconstitutional," sending proponents of teaching creation science in public schools scurrying for cover. Consequently, the Arkansas Board of Education attorneys were constantly on the defensive. Thus, the defense attorneys of the *McLean* case, from the beginning, allowed the ACLU's attorney to set a false, ahistorical paradigm of the constitutional limits regarding public religious expression. The ACLU's two-pronged attack against creation science (and, by extension, Christianity, which is the real issue) was as follows: (1) Creation science is religion because it relies on the Biblical account of creation while evolution is "pure" science; (2) since creation science is a religion, like all religions, it has no place in the public schools because it violates the Establishment Clauses of the First Amendment and is therefore patently unconstitutional. The ACLU, having laid this sophistic argument which the court and the defendant's having accepted such fallacious argumentation, the defendants were doomed to loose on appeal although they had both historical sanction and prior judicial precedent (*stare decisis*) on their side.

What evolutionists, liberals, and others hostile to Christian theistic for being the basis of the Constitution and the laws of the land have done through an intricate series of state and federal precedent-setting cases is dupe the American public into thinking that the so-called doctrine of "separation of church and state" means an aversion to any and everything even remotely Christian, or of a Christian influence (i.e., religion, Christian theism, morality, ethics). These ideas are not to be taught in the public schools or having any voice in the public marketplace. This type of constitutional law would have been utterly foreign to most jurists prior to World War II, and certainly such sophisms would have been considered tyrannical to the Framers of the Constitution and the founders of our great American republic.

The so-called doctrine of "separation of church and state" doesn't mean that church and state are *mutually exclusive,* but to the contrary, the two are mutually inclusive and are indivisible, thus impossible to separate. Even Jefferson, one of the most quoted by liberal revisionists in support of the mutually exclusivist view between church and state, consistently advocated, along with the overwhelming majority of the Framers, that religion was to be taught in the public schools as mandatory for maintaining public morality, a respect for the Christian religion, a knowledge of reading, literature, history, and science, most important, to a fledgling democracy. The Framers knew that unless a society had a sincere belief and reverence for God, any government created by man was doomed to fail. Church and state co-existed without judicial encroachment in America from the arrival of the *Mayflower* at Plymouth Rock in 1620[5] until the infamous *Engel* decision of 1962, by which a liberal activist Supreme Court, in conjunction with the declining moral values of American society and its growing hostility and intolerance of Christian theism, ruled prayer in the public schools unconstitutional.[6] However, as early as the late 1940s, beginning with the *McCollum* case,[7] the Court had gained sufficient momentum in the public area to label with impunity all teaching of the religion in a public school setting as being "clearly unconstitutional," so that by the time the lower federal court ruled on the *McLean* case, which favored "balanced treatment" of teaching creation science with evolution science, the case was easily dismissed without a jury, prompting the Arkansas Board of Education to appeal. With this new liberal constitutionalism firmly in place, the appeal by the defendants of the creation science view could be easily disparaged and stigmatized by the court as a patently religious doctrine and therefore unconstitutional. The *McLean* court heard very little scientific evidence supporting creation science philosophy because the court had already made up its mind that creation science was purely religious and thus unconstitutional.

 The *McLean* court, contrary to prior constitutional case law, used a broad, personalized definition of religion in order to cast as wide a net as possible in purging all expressions of Christianity from the public square. This trend had been started by liberal jurists as early as 1925, with the Scopes Monkey Trial victory. To the intellectual class and their willing accomplices in the press, this case was hyped to such an extent as not only a tremendous victory for evolution, but more importantly, a defeat against Christianity as the dominant moral and intellectual ideology in America. Shell-shocked from their "defeat," the church went into a full retreat from the political and intellectual realm until Jerry Falwell and his group, "The Moral Majority," helped secure the election of conservative Ronald Reagan in 1980.

In defining and distinguishing between creation and evolution science, the *McLean* court used a very broad definition of religion and a very narrow, exclusivistic definition of science. Key pejorative words such as "religion," "religious," "scientific," and "science" made an objective discussion or a neutral hearing of the two fields in an inclusive context entirely impossible. It is interesting to note that the *McLean* court could easily see the religious concepts of creation science but fail to see that inherently religious nature of our nation's most sacred documents to which the U.S. Constitution owes its origins. The court in *McLean* then cited its definition of science, followed by scientist Henry Morris's assertion of unilateral creative processes concerning the origins of life. The only "scientific" evidence supporting the creationist side that the court would allow was the work by Robert Gentry on radioactive polonium halos. However, even here, the court used very cursory terms in acknowledging its validity, stating that Gentry's discovery has been treated as a minor mystery that will eventually be explained (i.e., refuted or incorporated into the evolutionary doctrine).[8]

Another irony in this entire debate is that scientists have violated a cardinal rule of their own discipline: entering into the study of a theory with a rigid predisposition, namely, relegating their field of inquiry exclusively to the area of "naturalism" (i.e., materialism) and totally ignoring or impudently castigating a greater phenomenon: the "supernatural" or "metaphysical," which, contrary to liberals and evolutionists, can and has been put under the aegis of scientific inquiry and proven time and time again to be a viabler theory of origin. The defendants on the creation science side urged the plaintiffs to allow a *balanced treatment* of the teaching of the origins of the universe, advocating creation science as a viable and scientifically tenable alternative to evolution, both of which can be taught as competing scientific theories of the origins of life. Unfortunately, balanced treatment was not implemented because, among other mitigating factors, the *McLean* court used a rather narrow definition of "science" and a broad definition of "religion" to reach their conclusions. The *McLean* court ruled that creation science could not be taught in the public schools along with evolution science. The rationale is codified in the three statements below:

1. Creation science relied on the Genesis account of creation which by definition was considered a religion.
2. Since creation science is a religion, it would contravene the Establishment Clause of the First Amendment if taught in public schools;
3. Since creation science is a religion, or at least in large part based on religious beliefs, it could not be science because science only bases its hypotheses and conclusions solely on natural, not supernatural phenomenon.

Contrary to the opinion in *McLean,* there are numerous scientific evidences to validate creation science as both science and fact, the question of religion notwithstanding.[9] To add to the already anti-religious hysteria, on appeal the plaintiffs, represented by the ACLU, predicted numerous and ominous results of allowing church and state to become "entangled." This entanglement would occur if creation science were allowed to be taught in the public schools. This is a common ploy by liberals hostile to America's Judeo-Christian roots, by using such baseless assertions that it is unconstitutional for the church to be entangled with the state, to counter *any* mutual co-existence of church and state, which, incredibly, many liberal scholars claim was how the Framers intended church and state to exist! Not only does this view ignore volumes of historical evidence and constitutional precedent in the executive, legislative, and judicial branches, but total separation of church and state is quite impossible to implement comprehensively in any democratic society. For example, recent history has shown us that it was even impossible to achieve a unilateral separation of church and state under an overwhelmingly secularistic, totalitarian, regime such as communist Russia absent the brutal, repressive, and coercive tactics the government frequently used against its citizens—abridging their religious liberties. Even in totalitarian regimes like Russia, North Korea, Cuba, and China, "god" is the state; party members and bureaucrats, its high priests. So these atheistic regimes inevitably have the structure and hierarchy (albeit perversely) of religion.

The *McLean* court, contrary to its frequent denials, was not neutral concerning the matter of church and state relations, for the court, of necessity, must choose one religion over another—one ruling over another—a doctrine of atheism (evolution science) over a doctrine of theism (creation science). If the court does not discriminate, then any religious cult or sect, no matter how unorthodox, spurious, and dangerous its beliefs and inimical its practices to the public welfare, could gain legitimacy and protection under the Constitution. The Supreme Court (and, by extension, the *McLean* court), with its antithetical interpretation of the First and Fourteenth Amendments, regarding federal and state involvement with religion, has by judicial fiat virtually erased all vestiges of America's religious heritage of Christian theism from the public marketplace. Paradoxically, the courts have given legitimacy and First Amendment protection to many sects, cults, and other religious groups that have practices and beliefs antithetical to Christian theism. To this end, the ACLU has been most vigorous in convincing the courts that all forms of Christianity must be removed from the public forum lest the Establishment Clause be violated. As noted earlier, this is a form of constitutional law totally unknown prior to the 1940s. However, the ACLU then adamantly defends the "rights" of such religiously unorthodox groups as Satanists, the Ku Klux Klan, skinheads, neo-Nazis, Mormons, Moonies, Hare Krishna, etc. Herein lie the true ends of the ACLU and other liberal activist groups. It is not that they hate religion (although many liberals do); they just despise Christianity because they realize that this religion, apart from any other group or institution, has the moral grounding to destroy their philosophical base (liberalism) and the radical libertarian, radical egalitarian, and nihilistic philosophies that they have vigorously advocated since the early 1930s.

The *McLean* court cited efforts to try to make creation science "suitable" educationally and legally to be taught in the public schools. Marianne Wilson, director of science curriculum for Pulaski County Special School District, was asked by the district superintendent to produce a creation science curriculum guide for the Arkansas public schools. After reading all of the major writings of creation science, incredibly, she and her committee reached the conclusion that there wasn't enough creation science literature to form a curriculum guide.[10] Why? Because the liberal *McLean* court had painted creation science with such as broad brush, condemning it as religion, it then applied the second pretext of liberal law—that religion in the public schools is an unconstitutional violation of the Establishment Clause of the First Amendment.

Throughout the entire creation–evolution debate four premises are held as fact: (1) science is the closest thing to reality and truth known to mankind; (2) supernatural knowledge, *ipso facto* cannot be science but must be religion; (3) insistence that a belief system employ both religious and scientific concepts is a misconception and cannot exist; and (4) if one's philosophical base is religious or, more specifically, based on Christian theistic principles, then you have no public platform from which to justify your point of view. These four premises of science, which incredibly the court took for granted, are based on three common misconceptions about science and scientists: (1) scientists are objective; (2) scientists are unbiased; and (3) science is infallible. The court merely aped the contemporary liberal belief that science is omniscient: "If a scientist says it, it must be true." With this false paradigm firmly in place, the theistic status of creation science was summarily preempted by evolution science inquiry despite the frequent claims of the scientific community that science, by definition, is speculative and falsifiable. This view contrasts markedly with the orthodox view of Christian theism as practiced by the Framers, allowing no room for debate on its fundamental precepts such as freedom of religion, a pillar of constitutionalism in American law.

The *McLean* court used a narrow, mutually exlusivistic definition of science. By limiting boundaries of science and accepting a broad, all-encompassing definition of religion, the court in *McLean* contravened the spirit and letter of the religion clauses of the First and Fourteenth Amendments, citing the first clause ("Congress shall make no law respecting an establishment of religion") to contradict (and ultimately render void) the second clause ("nor prohibit the free exercise thereof"). That is why when reading Supreme Court decisions on the religion clauses of the Constitution over the past forty years, one realizes much has been said about violating the Establishment Clause, but very little analysis is expended by these same jurists on the free exercise clause. Nor do these judges seek to harmonize the Establishment Clause with (not against) itself as the Framers intended. This exclusivist view of church and state relations has also distorted and undermined the very Constitution, which protected Christian theistic principles in America for centuries. The liberal logic to justify this law works like this: In any court of law at any level, if one makes any reference to the Bible, God, or anything in a religious context, your entire thesis is summarily castigated, disparaged, and stigmatized as religious, synonymous with being void of educational, intellectual, critical, or scientific value. This shameful act of religious discrimination is expressly being advocated by the courts whose judges all swear to protect and defend the Constitution. A growing number of political scientists and, ironically, historians now believe the Constitution is a religious document based expressly on Judeo-Christian principles.

The real fear of the scientific community is that Christian theism will expose the foundation of scientific theory of evolution as being patently unscientific, untenable, and impossible.[11] Science feigns an open inquiry approach to all viable bodies of knowledge yet vehemently and unilaterally rejects creation science as a scientifically salient view of origins of life even though it received universal approbation by scientists from Galileo and Newton, to Linnaeus and Kepler, to Pasteur and Behe. Not until the publication of Darwin's *Origin of the Species* (1859) was scientific creationism seriously brought to doubt by the scientific and intellectual community. Historical evidence is ignored that there were many famous scientists, before and after Darwin, that believed in the creationist view of the origins of life, and their research and writings on this subject offered much more scientific proof than the evolution science side.[12]

In conclusion, the key holding of *McLean* was that evolution is not within the bounds of religion, but creation science is.[13] Not only is this not true, but a growing number of scientists, many with very impressive credentials, are reaching the conclusion that not only is evolution clearly a religion, but it is a false religion—slavishly adhered to as orthodoxy by the majority of scientists despite the mountain of evidence that evolution is physically and scientifically impossible. It takes a greater leap of faith to believe that the world was created by a large explosion billions of years ago than to believe that God created the universe out of nothing. The *McLean* court stressed the fact in reaching its decision that the Constitution is not governed by "public opinion polls or majority vote."[14] I beg to differ with the *McLean* court, historically, this republic was founded and its Constitution ratified by a majority of nine out of thirteen states in 1776.

In conclusion, there must be a "balanced treatment" of all constitutional rights, especially those contained in the Bill of Rights protecting an individual's freedom of religion, press, assembly, protest, etc. Otherwise the American public, along with its legal system will continue to slide into the abyss of freedom without restraint, compassion without conscience, liberty without freedom, and law without morality. The Scopes Monkey Trial and its progeny like *McLean* successfully used the scientific mythology of evolution to maintain its monopoly on intellectual thought regarding the scientific origins of life. This propaganda is taught from kindergarten through college. The theory of evolution, which is not mentioned in the First Amendment, is given judicial sanction, while the elements of creation science, which are expressly protected by the First Amendment, are treated as lepers and cast out of the public marketplace along with any beliefs whose origins are Christian. This type of liberal constitutionalism is insane and contrary to the Framers' original understanding of the Constitution, which clearly provided protection of religious liberties, specifically the teaching of creation science in the public schools. Creation science was taught for centuries in America long before Darwin's theory of evolution and even long before the advent of public education in America. History has shown us repeatedly that abridging religious liberties will lead to the eventual destruction of once great nations.[15] Unfortunately, the *McLean* opinion has taken us a step closer to the abyss.

Notes

1. *McLean v. Arkansas Board of Education,* 529 F. Supp., 1255 (1982). An Arkansas district court judge ruled against the "balanced treatment" approach supported by the Arkansas Board of Education, which would have permitted creation science to be taught equally with evolution science whenever evolution was taught in the public schools. 71. A. Act 590 of 1981, Ark., Stat. Ann. #80-1663, et seq. (1981 Supp.), "Balanced Treatment for Creation-Science and Evolution-Science Act." It was signed into law by President William Jefferson Clinton then governor of Arkansas, on March 19, 1981. A suit was brought against the constitutionality of Act 590 on May 27, 1981. Its premise was on three distinct grounds: "First, it is contended that Act 590 constitutes an establishment of religion prohibited by the First Amendment to the Constitution, which is made applicable to the states by the Fourteenth Amendment. Second, the plaintiffs argue the Act violates a right to academic freedom which they say is guaranteed to students and teachers by the Free Speech Clause of the First Amendment. Third, plaintiffs allege the Act is impermissibly vague and thereby violates the Due Process Clause of the Fourteenth Amendment." See *McLean,* at 1257. Excerpt of Federal Court Judge Overton's opinion in the *McLean* case, as quoted by L. Gilkey, *Creationism on Trial: Evolution and God at Little Rock 294* (1983).
2. *Scopes v. State,* 289 S.W. 363 (1925).
3. Genesis, chapters 1–11, contains the Biblical account of the origins of life in the world. This narrative is the foundation of creation science.
4. Justice Tom Clark, in the *Abington* decision, stated that "the State may not establish a 'religion of secularism,' " thus "preferring those who believe in no religion over those who do believe." (*Abington, 374 U.S. 205, 225 [1963].*) How can the Supreme Court be truly neu-

tral? *Sir Walter Moberly*, in *The Crisis in the University* (1949), comments on the religiously "neutral" British universities: "On the fundamental religions issue, the modern university intends to be, and supposes it is, neutral, but it is not. Certainly it neither inculcates nor expressly repudiates belief in God. But it does what is far more deadly than open rejection; it ignores Him. . . . It is in this sense that the university today is atheistic. . . . It is a fallacy to suppose that by omitting a subject you teach nothing about it. On the contrary, you teach that it is to be omitted, and that it is therefore a matter of secondary importance. And you teach this not openly and explicitly, which would invite criticism; you simply take it for granted and thereby insinuate it silently, insidiously, and all but irresistibly" (pp. 55–56).
5. See Mayflower Compact, November 11, 1620. The Pilgrims actually draft America's first constitution. It began thusly: "In The Name of God, Amen . . . Grace of God, . . . Defender of the Faith. Having undertaken for the Glory of God, and advancement of the Christian Faith, and the Honour of our King and Country, . . . " as quoted in *American Jurisprudence 2D Desk Book* 46 (1979).
6. *Engel v. Vitale,* 370 U.S. 421 (1962). The Supreme Court banned all state-required prayers in the public schools.
7. "Designed to serve as perhaps the most powerful agency for promoting cohesion among a heterogeneous democratic people, the public school must keep scrupulously free from entanglement in the strife of sects. The preservation of the community from divisive conflicts, of Government from irreconcilable pressures by religious groups, of religion from censorship and coercion however subtly exercised, requires strict confinement of the State to instruction other than religious, leaving to the individual's church and home, indoctrination in the faith of his choice" (*McCollum v. Board of Education,* 333 U.S. 203, 216–217 [1948]).
8. In summarizing Gentry's contributions, the court stated: "Robert Gentry's discovery of radioactive polonium haloes in granite and coalified woods is, perhaps, the most recent scientific work which the creationists use as argument for a 'relatively recent inception' of the earth and a worldwide food. The existence of polonium haloes in granite and coalified wood is thought to be inconsistent with radiometric dating methods based upon constant radioactive decay rates. . . . Gentry's discovery has been treated as a minor mystery which will eventually be explained" (529 F. Supp. 1270).
9. Paul Taylor, *The Illustrated Origins Answer Book* (1990) p. 7–8, 49–50. First Law of Thermodynamics: Energy can be changed from one form to another, but it cannot be created or destroyed. Second Law: When energy is being transformed from one state to another,

some of it is turned into energy that cannot be turned back into useful form, contrary to evolutionary theory, which presupposes that time passes all life will reach higher levels of complexity and development. However, the creationist theory correlates with both laws of thermodynamics, which postulate that all life is like a giant wound-up clock, slowly winding down. Scientists, especially for the past two centuries, have rediscovered thousands of ancient sites attesting to the Bible's accuracy. Archaeologists have found the Dead Sea Scrolls, which indisputably verified that the Bible was intact as late as the second century B.C., silencing liberal Bible scholars who held that most books of the Bible were written at a much later date than the Bible led us to believe. Noah's Ark was recently found by scientists. The ark's physical dimensions and present location (Mount Ararat) correlate exactly with the Biblical narrative. See R. Wyatt, *Discovered: Noah's Ark* (1989).

10. The results that Ms. Wilson and her committee reached after reading all creation science was that "all available creationists' materials [were] unacceptable because they were permeated with religious references and reliance upon religious beliefs" (529 F. Supp., 1270). The court stated the results of Ms. Wilson's and her committee's findings: "The curriculum guide which she prepared cannot be taught and has no educational value as science" (529. F. Supp., 1272).

11. In the sixth edition of his book *The Origin of the Species* (1872), Charles Darwin abandoned natural selection as the force behind evolution due to the continuing lack of evidence and theoretical problems (p. 66) The court in *McLean* stated: " . . . infringement by the defendants upon the academic freedom of teachers and students. . . . Teachers have been given freedom to teach and emphasize those portions of subjects the individual teacher considered important . . . the individual teacher should be permitted unlimited discretion subject only to the bounds of professional ethics. The court is not prepared to adopt such a broad view of academic freedom in the public schools" (*McLean supra,* note 71. A., at 1273).

12. To name a very few scientists, pre-and post-Darwin, who considered themselves creationists: Louis Agassiz, who helped develop the study of glacial geology and of ichthyology; Charles Babbage, who helped develop the science of computers and developed actuarial tables and the calculating machine; Francis Bacon, who developed the Scientific Method; Joseph Henry, who invented the electric motor and the galvanometer and discovered self-induction; William Hershel, who helped develop the science of galactic astronomy, discovered double stars, and developed the Global Star Catalog; James P. Joule, who developed reversible thermodynamics; Johann Kepler,

who helped develop the science of physical astronomy and developed the Ephemeris Tables; Carolus Linnaeus, who helped develop the sciences of taxonomy and systematic biology and developed the Classification System; Joseph Lister, who helped develop the science of antiseptic surgery; Gregor Mendel, founder of the modern science of genetics; Matthew Maury, who helped develop the science of electrodynamics; James Clerk Maxwell, who helped develop the science of electrodynamics; Isaac Newton, who helped develop the science of dynamics and the discipline of calculus, father of the Law of Gravity, and who invented the reflecting telescope; Louis Pasteur, who helped develop the science of bacteriology, discovered the Law of Biogenesis, invented fermentation control, and developed vaccinations and immunizations; Leonardo da Vinci, who helped develop the science of the hydraulics; Rudolf Virchow, who helped develop the science of pathology; and John Woodward, who helped develop the science of paleontology. See Paul Taylor, *The Illustrated Origins Answer Book* (p. 49). *McLean* stated: "Evolution is the cornerstone of modern biology, and many courses in public schools contain subject matter relating to such varied topics as the age of the earth, geology and relationships among living things. Any student who is deprived of instruction as to the prevailing scientific thought on these topics will be denied a significant part of science education."

13. The *McLean* court cited that the *Epperson v. Arkansas Board of Education*, 393 U.S. 97 (1968), decision was emphatic in its view in defining evolution: "that evolution is not a religion and that teaching evolution does not violate the Establishment Clause."
14. *McLean*, at 1274.
15. Judges 17:6. "In those days there was no King in Israel, but every man did that which was right in his own eyes." The most succinct summary of our Modern Age that I've ever read.

5

The Sophistry of Positive Law in Constitutional Jurisprudence

April 1, 1994

If there is any law which is back of the sovereignty of the state, and superior thereto, it is not law in such a sense as to concern the judge or lawyer, however much it concerns the statesman or moralist.[1]
—Benjamin Cardozo

If a judge can interpret the Constitution or laws to mean something obviously not intended by the original makers . . . then the nation's Constitution and laws are meaningless.[2]
—Lawrence P. McDonald

Introduction

Two narratives taken from the Bible will serve as a prelude to this Essay on positive law, it's major theorists, and the effect this philosophy has had and still holds on American jurisprudence and constitutional decision making. The first story is chronicled in chapter 32 of the book of Exodus.[3] The Israelites were in the wilderness of Sin *en route* to the Promise Land (Canaan). Moses was their leader, who through the power of God, delivered his people out of the bondage of slavery in Egypt where they had toiled for four hundred and thirty years.[4] God called Moses to Mount Sinai where he received from God what later became known as "The Ten Commandments." However, the Israelites grew impatient with Moses' absence, which lasted forty days, and forced his brother, Aaron, the High Priest, to "make us gods, which shall go before us; for as for this Moses, . . . we know not what is become of him."[5] Aaron capitulated to their demands and made them a golden calf from the earrings and jewelry they received from the Egyptians.[6] The Jews then worshiped their new "god" and even ascribed to him as the one which brought them out of Egypt.[7] When Aaron saw their devotion, he went further and built an altar for the idol and made an official proclamation that, "tomorrow is a feast to the Lord." Next, the Jews made sacrifices and offerings to their new god of gold and had a lavish banquet, which lead to a drunken orgy. God, being in the mountain with Moses, of course knew of their new "god" and tersely told Moses what had taken place— "thy people . . . have corrupted themselves." What makes this story so appropriate to our discussion here is that the Israelites, God's chosen people, had in a matter of a few days, changed from a law and legal principles based on the Ten Commandments of God to it's antithesis, a legal system on which all law presupposed a separation of law and morals, or a law where man's law and God's law aren't necessarily the same. How could the Jews, God's chosen people, who time after time had seen God's dramatic and unique displays of his power and purpose in their lives, so easily dismiss God and his prophet Moses and worship other gods? Secondly, this narrative should make it clear how fickle and capricious mankind can be in forsaking God's law of obedience to his commandments, for man's law of seeking his own interests and desires.

The second story is found in II Kings 21 and 22. Josiah was the eight year old boy-King of Judah (the southern part of

Israel). His father was the wicked King Manasseh who the Bible said, "did that which was evil in the sight of the Lord."[8] What did Manasseh do that was so blasphemous to God? He worshiped idol gods and all the planets of the heavens (astrology). He built altars to worship Satan (Baal worship). He practiced witchcraft, sorcery, and killed those who wanted to worship the true God. After 55 years of his ignoble reign, he was finally assassinated[9] and his son Josiah was made the new King. By now, the spiritual condition of Judah was deplorable, for Manasseh had diametrically opposed all that the law of Moses said to do. Josiah, aware of the dire spiritual condition of the people, began an ambitious program of rebuilding the temple and restoring the practices of true worship of God like their forefathers—Abraham, Isaac, and Jacob. During this rebuilding process, the high priest "found" a copy of the law of Moses (the first five books of the Bible). He gave it to Shaphan the scribe, who then read the book to the King. After the King heard the word of God, he rent his clothes—an ancient expression of profound sorrow and regret. The King immediately dispatched his priests and scribes to, "inquire of the Lord for me and for the people and for all Judah."[10] The King's envoy went to the prophetess Huldah, who told them that all of the evil written in the law of Moses which he heard will come to the people of Judah because they had forsaken God and his laws and have worshiped idol gods. But because King Josiah humbled himself and repented, the Lord would delay his judgment until after the King died. This narrative raises the pivotal question—How could one King so degenerate the moral and social conditions of an entire nation in just one generation? King Manasseh's father was Hezekiah, under whose reign brought the southern kingdom of Israel (Judah) to its greatest period of spiritual growth since the times of David and Solomon. King Hezekiah faithfully worshiped God, yet in just one generation, his son destroyed all that he had built by substituting a law based on the immutable principles of God (Judaism) for a law based on the constantly mutable laws of man (Baal worship).

What presuppositions are at the foundations of our laws? Our statutes? Our Constitution? Most legislators who write the laws, judges who interpret the laws, police, FBI, and other law similar organizations who enforce the laws, and lawyers who argue the law before courts and seek judicial redress to change the laws, have given little thought to these seemingly pivotal questions. If you understand law to be totally of human creation and human enforcement, you will have a very different approach to the law than someone whose understanding that all legitimate law is from a divine source (God) handed down to man to dispense equitably and justly according to a set of preordained, immutable principles codified in a written book (the Bible).

In this Essay, I would like to discuss one of the primary philosophical and intellectual suppositions that undergird our contemporary conceptions of *what the law is—positive law* or *legal positivism,* as opposed to *what the law ought to be—natural law* or *"the law of nature"* as philosopher John Locke and Thomas Jefferson understood it. This dichotomy has been much discussed by legal scholars as an argument both for and against positive law.[11] However, a growing number of critics seem unanimous in their assertion that the irreconcilable conflicts caused by positive law in constitutional jurisprudence greatly outweigh the problems positive law have purported to solve. To best understand positive law and its antecedents—*positivism* and *logical positivism,* you must understand their component meanings. *Positive law* simply means a law established or recognized by governmental authority. *Positivism* is a theory that theology and metaphysics are earlier imperfect modes of knowledge, and that positive knowledge is based on natural phenomena and their properties and relations as verified by the empirical sciences. *Logical positivism* was a philosophical movement that held characteristically that all meaningful statements are either analytic or conclusively verifiable, or at least confirmable by observation and experimentation and in regards to the law and its interpretation, metaphysical theories, (i.e., the Bible) are therefore strictly meaningless.

If one holds to the expressed presumption that all valid laws, ordinances, and precepts have separate and distinct legal and moral components, and you believe this is morally wrong, then the laws that the legislators and judges generate from these positive laws will likewise be morally wrong, corrupt, and ultimately destructive to society. For example, most people would agree that in our present system of government, we have more laws, statutes, and ordinances on the books than at any other time in history; and that tomorrow there will be more laws enacted than today. The great seventeenth-century philosopher John Hobbes referred to such a self-perpetuating government as, *Leviathan,* a terrible and dreadful sea monster mentioned in the Bible. This is the counterproductive effect of positive law. It seeks to fashion a law for the endless multiplicity of circumstances and situations rather than fashioning a general set of laws based on immutable principles that serve as the foundation of all other laws. Yet with all these laws, ordinances, and statutes we have on the books, escalating crime rates and increasing contempt for the law is higher than at anytime in the history of mankind. Why is this so? Ever since the second half of the nineteenth century, legality and morality have been systematically separated by scientists, intellectuals, philosophers, judges, legal theorists, and eventually adopted and enacted in legislative mandates and judicial opinions. Today, positive law and its progeny, positivism, legal positivism, and legal realism are the major philosophies of contemporary constitutional jurisprudence. Positive law is actually an outgrowth of an earlier eighteenth-century moral philosophy of *utilitarianism* from which early legal theorists derived their positive law theories. Utilitarianism is but one of several dozen or so modern secularist philosophies which all have their origins in relativism. What is relativism? R. H. Popkin, in his article on *Relativism* in *The Encyclopedia of Religion,* defines the core precepts of this philosophy:

> [V]iews are to be evaluated relative to the societies or cultures in which they appear and are not to be judged true or false, or good or bad, based on some overall criterion, but are to be assessed within the context in which they occur. Thus, what is right or good or true to one person or group, may not be considered so by others . . . there [are] no absolute standards. . . . "Man is the measure of all things", and . . . each man could be his own measure. . . . Cannibalism, incest, and other practices considered taboo are just variant kinds of behavior, to be appreciated as acceptable in some cultures and not in others. . . . [Relativism] urges suspension of judgment about right or wrong. . . .[12]

John Dewey, the father of modern public education in America, insisted on relativism as the basis for public education. In his book, *The Public and Its Problems,* Dewey stated that, "The belief in political fixity, of the sanctity of some form of state consecrated by the efforts of our fathers and hallowed by tradition, is one of the stumbling-blocks in the way of orderly and directed change."[13] Historians Dornan and Vedlik in their book, *Judicial Supremacy,* noted that Justices ascribing to relativism in their jurisprudence rejected the natural law doctrine the Framers used in writing the Constitution:

> The natural law and natural rights principles which [earlier Justices] had also been reading into the Constitution . . . were not applicable to a society that was in a constant state of flux and change. . . . But in the process, the idea of transcendent rights

would be discarded, and there would be no appeal from the edicts of the true law-giver—the Court. Government would become the sole source of rights.[14]

Origins of Legal Positivism

Although the use of the word positive law can be traced as far back as the fourteenth century, it did not develop into an independent, coherent legal theory until the late eighteenth and early nineteenth centuries. Historically, this also corresponded to the height of the secular revival movement called the Enlightenment. During this time men of learning consciously sought to discover knowledge solely through the use and development of their own faculties, apart from acknowledging any divine source. The two major theorists of legal positivism were the British philosophers John Austin[15] and Jeremy Bentham.[16] The common theme throughout their writings insisted that "law as it is" is not necessarily the same as "law as it should be." In other words, law and morals are distinct entities. Positivism is actually an outgrowth of *utilitarianism* or a view of moral life that regard the consequences of an act demonstrative of what is good or morally right. Throughout the writings of Austin and Bentham are presuppositions toward a utilitarian moral outlook.[17] Bentham and Austin believed that a law, ordinance, statute, or even a Constitution, could be perfectly valid law apart from any pre-existing moral precepts. For example, Bentham believed that a law is right or good if it brings the most happiness (or least unhappiness) to most people. Bentham called this the "*Principle of Utility*," and he frequently used it to evaluate laws from a moral point of view. This insistence on an expressed segregation between morality and legality was further developed by predecessors of Austin and Bentham and became known as the *separability thesis*. Thus, throughout their writings, the expressed descriptions and examples of what law is—"expository" or "analytical" jurisprudence and what law ought to be—"censorial" or "normative" jurisprudence, was consistently demonstrable.

Hart's Theory of Positive Law

Oxford philosophy professor and Harvard lecturer, H. L. A. Hart, in his famous essay, *Positive Law and the Separation of Law and Morality,* defends positivism against a then growing number of critics. Hart's thesis held that the critics of positive law confuse two core positivism precepts—the *separability thesis*—legality separate from morality, and Austin's *command doctrine*—law as a command by a sovereign enforced by a threat. Hart later agreed with his critics that Austin's command doctrine was too riddled with inconsistencies to be considered a serious legal theory. However, the critics then deduced that since the command doctrine is theoretically invalid, so must be the entire positive law philosophy. Hart's solution to this dilemma was to retain positive law's separability thesis doctrine and reject Austin's command doctrine model as theoretically untenable. Hart is credited with codifying the positivism theories of Austin and Bentham into a coherent legal philosophy applicable in contemporary jurisprudence. His major work on positive law is the book, *The Concept of Law* (1961) and an essay, "*Positivism and the Separation of Law and Morals*" (1958), of which the latter will serve as a major focal point in this Essay. In his essay, Hart makes two major premises: (1) to clarify the essential positivism elements of the separability of law and morals; (2) to defend positivism's major tenant—the separability thesis against charges of the critics.

Since Austin and Bentham are the two positive law theorists Hart concentrates on, it will be useful to describe a few terms they used before analyzing his article. Austin believed that *law* is a *command.* A *command* is a signification of desire backed by a credible threat of punishment, a threat that if necessary, can be enforced. Not everyone's command is law. The command of the *"sovereign"* is the only certifiable law to Austin. What made Austin's sovereign unique and provocative to the Victorian sensibilities of his day was that it wasn't defined in religious, normative, or moral terms, such as "he who has the right to rule," or "he who legitimately rules." Instead, Austin argued that the sovereign is that person, or group of persons, which has the most people obeying them and conversely is generally under no obligation to obey anyone else—"the unobeying obeyed." So, if person X is generally obeyed by the majority of the population and yet does not in fact generally obey anyone else, then that person is the sovereign. Indispensable to Austin's sovereign is the ability to enforce its commands. Without the ability to enforce his commands, one could not be a sovereign and his word wouldn't be considered law.

Hart, though a positivist, expressly rejected one of the core precepts of Austin's positive law precepts—the command doctrine, which Hart said, "was breathtaking in its simplicity and quite inadequate."[18] To further bolster his argument, Hart poses a series of questions—Do all laws fit this model—law as a desire backed by a credible threat? In criminal law, yes; in contracts, wills, and constitutional law, no![19] If one wishes to enter into a contract with someone, or to draft a will to benefit a family member, there is no "command" in an Austinian sense that is compelling. But instead, the law has procedures and statutes one must follow in order to give effect to the document. For example, to have a valid contract, one should put in all relevant terms (i.e., description of goods, quantity, time, place of delivery, parties, cost, etc.). Likewise, in wills, if one wishes to give certainty and effect to the dispensation of his property, *post mortem,* one should expressly state this intent in a written document (will or trust). To Austin, not obeying these rules, or complying with the statutes controlling contracts and wills, would trigger a "sanction of nullity"—the sovereign authority will not give effect to my will or contract because I didn't follow the proper procedures.

How would Austin's command doctrine apply to constitutional law? The Constitution doesn't expressly command anyone to obey it at the threat of punishment. Theoretically speaking, our present Constitution could be voided and an entirely new Constitution ratified by Congress if they got a two-thirds majority vote in the Senate and the House of Representatives. Thus, it is possible that our present Constitution could no longer be the foundation of all laws in the United States. This is not to denigrate the fact that the Constitution is "law," or that it isn't law in the Austinian sense of a command of the sovereign backed by enforceable threat or punishment. The Constitution is rather a system of laws based on a specific philosophy that in 1789 a majority of nine of the thirteen colonies ratified to become the supreme law of the land in protecting certain fundamental rights of the people and expressly limiting the powers of the three branches of the federal government, the presidency, the legislature and the judiciary.

Other problems arise with Austin's narrow conception of sovereignty. Who is the sovereign of the U.S.? The President? The Congress? The Supreme Court? "We the people?" If anyone of these entities are the sovereign, then what are the others? Would Austin's sovereign allow a modification of his model in place of, for example, a system of government where the people (individually and collectively) choose representatives in their stead to be the sovereign? (i.e., Hobbes' social contract theory). A strict reading of Austin's command theory would not allow such a modification because the moment a sovereign gave up or lost his power to rule, he would no longer be a sovereign power for few people would feel any obligation to obey him. This would be true whether one is speaking of a social contract as in the Western democratic model, or a fascist, totalitarian, or communist regime, where the "state" clearly is the sovereign and "the people" are mere cogs in the machinery of the state with little or no individual rights, liberties, or freedoms. Finally, can sovereigns issue commands to themselves? To do this, one would have to differentiate between "official" and "unofficial capacity." Austin's model makes no concession to this ideal. Austin only recognizes those people who are generally obeyed (sovereigns) and those who are under the sovereign's law (everyone else).

Positive Law's "Frequent Coincidences" with Natural Law

In his famous Essay, *Positivism and the Separation of Law and Morality,* Hart analyses several arguments against a legal theory that presupposes that legality and morality are two different issues. Strong, clear, moral principles must undergird all law, for some laws are so general that it is difficult to determine their proper application. For example, Hart cites the law "No vehicles in the park" as a prima facie case for a union between law and morals,[20] for one cannot determine whether a mini-bike versus "bicycles, roller skates, or toy autos," would be permissible without employing moral judgments. Critics then argue that positive law must frequently join legality to morality by agreeing that the law is valid to protect people at the park from getting hit by a motor vehicle, and to allow a mini-bike, though a "vehicle," would contravene the spirit and letter of the law. For positivism to hold otherwise would be to commit "the error of formalism"—the understanding that all rules can be clearly applied to any given set of facts with "complete logical certainty." Hart says that "the misconceptions of the judicial process which ignores the problems of the penumbra and which views the process as consisting pre-eminently in deductive reasoning is often stigmatized as the error of "formalism" or "literalism."[21] Hart counters that the critics have created a false dilemma—for one can follow the separability thesis and not use moral principles to interpret the law—"No vehicles in the park"—without succumbing to the formalistic logic in resolving these "penumbra" or "fuzzy" cases by relying on what Hart refers to as the "social policies, traditions, or customs of the community" (i.e., Biblical precepts). To cover this glaring contradiction, Hart seemingly thwarts his critics with a retreat to the philosophy utilitarianism. Utilitarianism looks at laws not from a normative or moral perspective, but in purely humanistic or social terms. A good law is determined by its consequences and its ultimate affect (i.e., utility) on the majority of the population in a given community. Hart's attempt here to confront his critics rings hollow, for he totally ignores the undeniable historical fact that in every civilization since Adam and Eve, the "social policies, traditions and customs" were generally: (a) normative and objective in nature, and (b) had their ultimate origins in some religious-based belief system which is the foundation of all morality.

Secondly, critics of positivism look to examples of history to see what can happen when law is separated from morals. The most frequently cited example was the Nazi regime.[22] By all accounts, the Third Reich was truly an evil empire. Yet they had a rule of law (*rechstaat*) which the German people lived under, even though it was definitely immoral compared to their past "traditions, customs and social policies." (Remember that Germany was the birthplace of the Christian revivalist movement called the Protestant Reformation.) Critics argue that positive law's insistence on the separation of law and morals, even if the "law" is clearly immoral, allowed easy exploitation by the Nazis and other totalitarian regimes, because once law is separated from its religious/moral foundations, anarchy and moral collapse will quickly fill the void. This is because law has no intrinsic conscience or coherence in its own right—humans give a conscience to the law. Nazism striped the law of its conscience by replacing the God of the Bible with an idol god of man's creation—*die Fuhrer,* who represented the absolute supremacy of the State. Thus, the Nazi's use of positive law opened the floodgates to despotism and tyranny filling the vacuum that the morally corrupt and weak Weimar Republic failed to do. Hart tries to counter these arguments by his insistence on keeping the separability thesis, while rejecting Austin's command doctrine, before finally capitulating repeatedly to a primary thesis of natural law—**[some laws are just too morally outrageous to be legitimately recognized as law]**.

Finally, Hart makes a third concession, or what Austin calls a "frequent coincidence"[23] in favor of natural law jurisprudence. Hart states that, "It is not in fact always easy to trace this historical causal connection, but Bentham was certainly ready to admit its existence; so too Austin spoke of the 'frequent coincidence' of positive law and morality and attributed the confusion of what law is with what law ought to be to this very fact."[24] Hart and other positivists cannot ignore the fact that an indispensable component of every legal system at least is some minimal degree of moral content. Hart uses as an example the necessity of laws to protect people against physical violence. Hart acknowledges natural law's superiority in this area, but quickly cautions us not to mistake the "necessity" for such laws for a "truth" about the nature of law. This reasoning is incongruous because it seeks credence from a legal theory which by definition it is diametrical to, then stubbornly and illogically refuses to acknowledge the core principle of natural law—**God as the only foundation of all legitimate laws.**

Positivism and Rules

Hart, in his book, *The Concept of Law*,[25] sought to revise positivism by further correcting some of the implicit contradictions of Austin's theory. To Austin, law was viewed in purely coercive terms which Hart called, "the gunman situation writ large." To this view, Hart sought to correct what he perceived to be Austin's misconception of law by distinguishing between a law where, for example, you are obliged to give your money to a robber to avoid physical harm, and a law in which we are legally obligated to pay our taxes by April 15 to avoid a penalty. Feeling obliged and being obligated are two very different psychological states that Austin's positive law philosophy failed to distinguish between. Hart characterized his theory of positivism by stating that law is a system of *primary* and *secondary* rules. Primary rules govern the way people live and behave. They are social in nature. "No one may drive faster that 55 mph" and "Pay your taxes by April 15" are examples of primary rules. Secondary rules, conversely, aren't concerned with human conduct, but with the rules themselves. "The traffic code is exclusively the jurisdiction of the State," and "proposed changes in the tax code must be approved by Congress" are two examples Hart cites. The differences between primary and secondary rules are further developed by Hart in his notion of the rule of recognition, which says that primary rules must be supplemented, supported, and defined by secondary rules. This is what Hart means by such phrases as, "Whatever the chief utters is law," or "Whatever the legislatures enact consistently with the Constitution is law," as examples of rule recognition.

Stanley Paulson, in his article, *Classical Legal Positivism at Nuremberg*,[26] criticizes positivism's inability to effectively deal with immoral legal regimes like Nazi Germany. During the Nuremberg trials, this fact became acute as it developed that the primary defense of the Nazi war criminals would be an appeal to none other than Austin's doctrine of the sovereign holding that where two entities are deemed sovereign, (here the Allied governments vs. Germany), there can be no laws between them that either entities are obliged to comply with. To do otherwise, neither would be sovereign. Thus, the defendants, by evoking the positive law doctrine of the sovereign, tried to escape culpability for their war crimes reasoning that Germany, as a sovereign nation, cannot be governed by any other laws but those of Germany. Secondly, the defendant's argued that because Austin's command doctrine required strict obedience—Bentham says, "to censure freely, to obey punctually."[27] Thirdly, the defendants claimed that they had no choice but to comply with the orders of their superiors. Such sophisms, though superficially compelling, proved morally spurious, misleading, and untrue. In the end, all of the twenty-four Nazi defendants were either executed or given life sentences in prison. In rebuttal against these defenses, U.S. Supreme Court Justice Charles Jackson, the lead prosecutor for the U.S. at the Nuremberg trials, sounded a strong natural law precept countering the defendants' contention that they had no choice but to obey orders, when he inquired—"Does it take these men by surprise that murder is treated as a crime?"[28] To the adherents of positive law, the answer is yes; to those of a natural law view, the answer is absolutely not!

Natural Law and the Constitution

The dominant philosophical theory of most Western governments that also served as the foundation of their legal systems was natural law, or "the law of nature." Natural law traces its origins back to the ancient Greeks and Romans. Catholic theologian Thomas Aquinas codified the natural law philosophies of Aristotle, Plato, and Cicero into a coherent demonstrable set of principles by which the burgeoning city states of Western Europe would later use as models for their systems of government. Aquinas, in his magnum opus, *Summa Theologica,* held that there were actually four types of law: *Eternal, Divine, Natural* and *Human.*[29] *Eternal law* was God's general plan for all creation. *Divine law* was the expressed commands of God found in the Bible. A strict adherence of divine law for Aquinas was indispensable to any government of man. Natural law was the only philosophy that recognized man's fallen and sinful nature which needed redemption by appeal to a "higher" law (i.e., God's revealed word in the Bible). Aquinas believed that only as man subjected himself and his laws to the laws of God, could his natural propensities toward selfishness, violence, and anarchy be abated. Aquinas understood that mere intellect or reason alone would be inadequate to make man govern himself (as positive law advocates believe) but humanity's fallen and evil nature must be tempered by the Word of God to **make** him do the right thing. *Human law* is a creation of humans to govern the requirements of natural law. *Natural law* for Aquinas was the application of God's eternal law to our human law, or more specifically, the application of God's divine law [the Bible] to human law. This is so because Aquinas believed that since God created the universe and everything in it, he likewise created mankind for a unique and specific purpose quite different from the rest of nature. All creation is therefore under God's providence and are "ruled and measured" by God's authority.

What are the requirements of natural law? Aquinas uses Aristotle to answer this question, for it was Aristotle's writings on natural law that first distinguished between two different types of reason—*speculative* and *practical. Speculative reason* is our unique understanding of the universe to formulate theories about certain truths. For example, the principles of math can help everyone from balancing a check book to constructing a skyscraper. However, practical reason deals with more concrete issues of life—love, family, honor, civility, religion. Both Aristotle and Aquinas held that in speculative and practical reason, certain truths are so foundational and immutable as to be *"per se nota"*—known through themselves or self-evident. A self-evident truth is unilaterally true in and of itself and not derivable from anything. Aquinas's principle of noncontradiction is an example of a self-evident principle of speculative reason which holds, "what is is and what is not, is not," as well as general principles of math and science. Examples of Aquinas's principles of practical reasoning include the precepts of natural law— "good is to be done and evil avoided," and "God's precepts are to be obeyed."

Since the tower of Babel,[30] mankind has recognized the indispensable need to govern himself. With each established government, there must be some undergirding philosophical basis to give that government consistency, coherence, legitimacy, and authority.[31] Law professor Lon Fuller calls this concept *Fidelity to Law*. For example, historians Dornan and Vedlik stated that:

> the Constitution is not a neutral document but presupposes a belief in a transcendent, unchanging order, and the cause behind that order: God. The Constitution is founded on the conviction that these rights are endowed by the Creator. The Constitution in short, is not a positivistic document but presupposes and is deeply rooted in theism. This is only natural for the men who framed the Constitution were all theists—mostly Christians, some deists.[32]

In other words, mankind has had very specific reasons for creating the types of government that have come down through the ages. Never in the history of man has any government that was of any significance been established by haphazard or improvisational means. The Framers of the U.S. Constitution, in their creation of a "Republic," were no different. They purposely and deliberately infused a clear and coherent natural law philosophy into the Constitution. The Constitution, along with the Declaration of Independence and the Bill of Rights, all are natural law documents. To underscore this fact, during the Constitutional Convention Ben Franklin stated that there has always been a multitude of philosophies that governments have been founded on but "We have gone back to ancient history for models of government, and examined the different forms of those Republics which having been formed. . . . And we have viewed Modern States all around Europe." [33]

Most historians seem to be in agreement that the Framers, in writing the Constitution, examined numerous and widely differing types of philosophies as they searched for a government that would be enduring, just, prosperous, and successful for all. What philosophy did the Framers choose to be the foundation of this new government? John Eidsmoe cites a study by political science professors Donald S. Lutz and Charles S. Hyneman in which they reviewed approximately 15,000 items and carefully read nearly 2,200 books, pamphlets, newspaper articles, and monographs, emphasizing expressed citations of political content printed between 1760 and 1805. After this material was compiled, read and sorted, they noted the philosophers quoted most frequently by the Framers—(1) Baron Charles Montesquieu, (2) Sir William Blackstone, and (3) John Locke.[34] What did these three men write that so greatly influenced the Framers as they drafted the Declaration of Independence, the Constitution, and the Bill of Rights? George Bancroft, in his book, *History of the United States,* quotes from Montesquieu's book, *The Spirit of Law* (1748) as having had a tremendous influence on the Framers in their search for the proper type of government for the colonies when he wrote, "society, notwithstanding all its revolutions, must repose on principles that do not change."[35] Montesquieu, in a seemingly prophetic manner, noted that the very revolution that would occur in France a generation later would be in vain unless the government that replaced the existing monarchy was founded on immutable moral principles. What principles and laws did Montesquieu have in mind for the successful government? Montesquieu answers the question:

> The Christian religion, which ordains that men should love each other, would, without doubt, have every nation blest with the best civil, the best political laws; because these, next to this religion, are the greatest good that these men can give and receive.[36]

On Blackstone, J. Thornton, wrote in his book, *The Pulpit of the American Revolution,* that, "I hear that they have sold nearly as many of Blackstone's Commentaries in America as in England." Blackstone's *magnum opus* is his celebrated treatise, *Commentaries on the Laws of England*[37] (1769). James Madison, the third President of the U.S., stated in a letter he wrote to a friend in 1821 that, "I very cheerfully express my approbation of the proposed edition of Blackstone's *Commentaries.*"[38] In Dornan and Vedlik's book, *Judicial Supremacy, The Supreme Court on Trial,* the authors noted, "It was from Blackstone that most Americans, including John Marshall, acquired their knowledge of natural law. . . . Blackstone remained the standard manual of law until the publication of *The Commentaries on American Law* (1826–1830) of Chancellor James Kent of New York."[39] Blackstone, in his *Commentaries,* stated:

> Man, considered as a creature, must necessarily be subject to

the laws of his creator, for he is entirely a dependent being. . . . And consequently, as man depends absolutely upon his maker for everything, it is necessary that he should in all points conform to his maker's will. This will of his maker is called the law of nature.[40]

Blackstone further noted:

> This law of nature . . . dictated by God himself, is of course superior in obligation to any other. . . . No human laws are of any validity, if contrary to this; . . . The revealed or divine law . . . found only in the holy scriptures . . . are found upon comparison to be really a part of the original law of nature[41] that, upon these two foundations, the law of nature and the law of revelation, depend all human laws; that is to say, no human laws should be suffered to contradict these.[42] To instance in the case of murder: this is expressly forbidden by the divine, and demonstrably by the natural law; and, from these prohibitions, arises the true unlawfulness of this crime. . . . If any human law should allow or enjoin us to commit it, we are bound to transgress that human law, or else we must offend both the natural and the divine. But, with regard to matters that are . . . not commanded or forbidden by [the Scriptures]—such, for instance, as exporting of wool into foreign countries,—here the . . . legislature [of men] has scope and opportunity to interpose, and to make that action unlawful which before was not so.[43]

John Locke's ideas on government were greatly influenced by the great English theologian and writer Richard Hooker. Hooker argued that where the Scripture is clear, Scripture alone must govern. Where Scripture is unclear . . . tradition may be employed to help interpret it; and where both Scripture and . . . tradition are unclear, or where new circumstances arise, reason may also be employed to apprehend God's truth.[44] Hooker further noted that, "The idea that men in a state of nature realize their rights are insecure, and compact together to establish a government and cede to that government certain power so that government may use that power to secure the rest of their rights."[45] And "Only the power of God and/or people delegate." This is the cornerstone of limited government. It finds expression in the Tenth Amendment to the Constitution and in the Declaration of Independence, which states that governments exist to secure human rights and "derive their just powers from the consent of the governed."[46] David Barton noted of Locke, "In his *First Treatise on Government,* he cited the Bible eighty times. . . . Twenty-two biblical citations appear in his second treatise. . . . His basic doctrines of parental authority, private property, and social compact were based on the historical existence of Adam and Noah." Locke stated in his *Second Treatise on Civil Government,* that "[t]hus the Law of Nature stands as an eternal rule to all men, legislators as well as others. The rules that they make for other men's actions, must . . . be conformable to the Law of Nature, i.e., to the will of God . . . no human sanction can be good, or valid against it;"[47] and, "Laws human must be made according to the general laws of Nature, and without contradiction to any positive of Scripture, otherwise they are ill made."[48] Through the writings of Montesquieu, Blackstone, and Locke on law and politics, the natural law philosophy was throughly influential in the minds of America's Framers, and that philosophy was widely held as being the best philosophy that a government could be founded upon. Thus, by these and many other like-minded writers, the Framers of the Constitution found ample evidence of the virtues of the natural law philosophy they would eventually choose as the controlling philosophy of the Constitution in America.

Notes

1. Benjamin Cardozo, *The Growth of the Law,* Yale University Press, New Haven, CT, p. 49, 1924. Cited by David Barton, *The Myth of Separation: What Is the Correct Relationship Between Church and State?*, WallBuilder Press, Aledo, TX, 1992, p. 205.
2. Lawrence P. McDonald, *We Hold These Truths,* '76 Press, Seal Beach, CA, 1976, p. 32.
3. All biblical references are taken from the authorized standard King James Version of the Bible (1611). According to an exhaustive study by two professors of history—Donald S. Lutz and Charles S. Hyneman, who reviewed over 15,000 printed items from 1760–1805 and discovered that the Bible accounted for 34% of all the Founder's direct quotes. See Donald Lutz, *The Origins of American Constitutionalism,* Louisiana State University Press, Baton Rouge, LA, 1988, p. 141. Another 60% of their quotes were drawn from authors who had derived their ideas from the Bible. Therefore, it can be shown that 94% of their quotes are based either directly or indirectly on the Bible. See Stephen McDowell and Mark A. Beliles, *America's Providential History,* Providence Press, Charlottesville, VA, 1989, p. 186. Also see Woodward and Gates, "How the Bible Made America," *Newsweek,* December 27, 1982, p.44, "historians are discovering that the Bible, perhaps even more than the Constitution, is our Founding document."
4. Exodus 12:40, "Now the sojourning of the children of Israel, who dwelt in Egypt, was four hundred and thirty years."
5. Exodus 32:1.
6. Ibid., 32:2–4.
7. Ibid., 32:4.
8. II Kings 21:1.
9. Ibid., 21:23 "And the servants of Amon conspired against him (Manasseh), and slew the King in his own house."
10. Ibid., 22:13.
11. Brecht, "The Myth of Is Ought," *Harvard Law Review,* 54 (1941), p. 811; H. L. A. Hart, "Positivism and the Separation of Law and Morals," *Harvard Law Review,* 71, (1958), p. 593; Lon Fuller, "Positivism," *Harvard Law Review,* 71, (1958), p. 630; Lon Fuller, *Anatomy of the Law,* Praeger, New York, 1968, pp. 175–85.
12. *The Encyclopedia of Religion,* "Relativism" by Richard H. Popkin, Macmillan Publishing Co., NY, 1987. Cited by Barton, p. 202.
13. John Dewey, the father of modern public education in America, insisted on relativism as the basis for public education. See John Dewey, *The Public and Its Problems,* Henry Holt, NY, 1927, p. 4,

"The belief in political fixity, of the sanctity of some form of state consecrated by the efforts of our fathers and hallowed by tradition, is one of the stumbling-blocks in the way of orderly and directed change."
14. Justices ascribing to relativism in their jurisprudence, rejected the natural law doctrine the Framers used in writing the Constitution. Also see Robert K. Dornan and Csaba Vedlik, Jr., *Judicial Supremacy: The Supreme Court on Trial*, Plymouth Rock Foundation, MA, 1986, p. 26.
15. John Austin, *The Providence of Jurisprudence Determined*, Library of Ideas, London, 1954, pp. 185–86.
16. Jeremey Bentham, "A Fragment on Government," in *I Works*, Bowring, London, 1859, p. 221.; "Principles of Penal Law," in *I Works*, Bowring, London, 1859, p. 865; "Of Promulgation of the Law," in *I Works*, Bowring, London, 1859, p. 297; "Principles of Morals and Legislation," in *I Works*, Bowring, London, 1859, p. 84, c. XIII.
17. Hart, *Positivism*, pp. 594–95.
18. Ibid., p. 602.
19. Ibid., p. 604.
20. Ibid., p. 607.
21. Ibid., p. 608.
22. Ibid., pp. 616–20.
23. Ibid., pp. 598–99 (footnote omitted).
24. David Adams, *Philosophic Problems in the Law*, Wadsworth Publishing Co., Belmont, CA, 1992, p. 27.
25. H. L. A. Hart, *The Concept of the Law*, Clarendon Press, Oxford, England, 1961.
26. Stanley Paulson, "Classical Legal Positivism at Nuremberg," *4 Philosophy & Public Affairs* (1975), p. 132.
27. Bentham, *Fragment*, p. 230.
28. Adams, *Philosophical Problems in the Law*, p. 12.
29. See generally, Thomas Aquinas, *Summa Theologica, The Basic Writings of Saint Thomas Aquinas*, Vol. 2, Random House, NY, 1945, p. 742.
30. Genesis 11:1–4.
31. Alexander Hamilton, *The Papers of Alexander Hamilton*, February 23, 1775, Columbia University Press, NY, 1961, Vol. 1, p. 86, taken from his "The Farmer Refuted": "Apply yourself, without delay, to the study of the law of nature. I would recommend to your perusal, Grotius, Pufendorf, Locke, Montesquieu; John Eidsmoe, in his seminal work, *Christianity and the Constitution*, Baker Book House, MI, 1987, p. 61, Hugo Grotius (1583-1645), [was a] famous Dutch lawyer, theologian, statesman. . . . In his writings on law and government, Grotius attempted to apply Christian principles to politics. He emphasized, perhaps more clearly than any other writer, that "what

God has shown to be his will that is law."

Ibid., Barton, *The Myth of Separation,* p. 65, "Samuel de Pufendorf was Professor of the Law of Nature, first at the University of Heidelberg (1661–1668) and then at the University of Lund in Sweden. He became the royal historian for Sweden. . . . Pufendorf, influenced by Grotius, helped to established the law of nature as the basis for international law;"

Ibid., Barton, *The Myth of Separation,* pp. 66–67, "Alexander Hamilton, Benjamin Franklin, James Wilson, Samuel Adams and other founding fathers paid tribute to Pufendorf, acknowledged his influence on their thinking, and recommended his writings to others."

George Mason, author of Virginia's Bill of Rights in its Constitution, stated before the General Court of Virginia, "The laws of nature are the laws of God, whose authority can be superseded by no power on earth." It was in this context that the phrase, "the laws of nature and nature's God," was subsequently incorporated in the Declaration of Independence. See Russ Walton, *Biblical Principles of Importance to Godly Christians,* Plymouth Rock Foundation, NH, 1984, p.358.

32. Dornan and Vedlik, *Judicial Supremacy,* p. 70, "The Constitution is not a neutral document but presupposes a belief in a transcendent, unchanging order, and the cause behind that order: God. It is founded on the conviction that these rights are endowed are by the Creator. The Constitution in short, is not a positivistic document but presupposes and is deeply rooted in theism. This is only natural, for the men who framed the Constitution were all theists—mostly Christians, some deists."
33. James Madison, *The Record of The Federal Convention,* New Haven, CT, (1911), Vol. I, pp. 91, 451, June 28, 1787.
34. Eidsmoe, *Christianity and the Constitution,* pp. 51, 53.
35. Charles Bancroft, *Bancroft's History of the United States,* Little Brown & Co., Boston, 1859, Vol. I, p. 24.
36. Charles Montesquieu, *The Spirit of The Laws,* Isaiah Thomas, Worcester, MA, 1802, Vol. I, pp. 125–26.
37. J. Wingate Thorton, "The Pulpit of The American Revolution," Gould & Lincoln, Boston, 1860, p. XXVII; William Blackstone's *magnum opus* is his celebrated treatise, *Commentaries on the Laws of England,* Clarendon Press, Oxford, 1769.
38. James Madison, *Letters and Other Writings of James Madison,* R. Worthington, NY, 1802, Vol. III, letter dated October 18, 1821.
39. Dornan and Vedlik, *Judicial Supremacy,* p. 10.
40. Blackstone, *Commentaries,* Vol. I, p. 39.
41. Ibid., Vol. I, pp. 41–42.

42. See Id. At Vol. I, p. 42.
43. Ibid.
44. Cited by Barton, *The Myth of Separation,* p. 198.
45. Ibid.
46. Ibid., pp. 198–99.
47. John Locke, *The Second Treatise on Civil Government,* Prometheus Books, Buffalo, NY, 1968, p. 75.
48. Ibid., p. 76.

6
Constitutional Crisis

Why is the Supreme Court, our nation's highest judicial body and the final arbiter of how the Constitution is interpreted, in a constitutional crisis? Is it because the philosophies it decides cases by were not the philosophy the Framers intended to interpret the Constitution? It is my contention that the answer is yes. There is no *fit* in applying positive law to an intrinsically natural document such as the Constitution. This constitutional crisis is evidenced by the fact that a sitting Court one year can hold a decision "constitutional," only to have it ruled a few years later "unconstitutional" by another Court. This type of jurisprudence is absurd because there is no stability or predictability in the law. A pivotal question is what judicial philosophy does the Supreme Court use to guide them in their decision making, or in interpreting the Constitution? Do judges make up their jurisprudence as they go along? Do words like *stare decisis,* original intent, Christianity, Framers, naturalism, or judicial activism, mean anything to modern jurists? Is the Court concerned about abiding by these doctrines? Which ones? Why? Why not others? These and many other questions come to mind when reading any of a number of Court decisions, especially those opinions regarding normative issues and principles.

Since 1960, traditional practices of morality, family values, and religious or Christian influence in the public domain that the Court long held as constitutional and beneficial for society, began to be systematically struck down as unconstitutional by a liberal activist Supreme Court that was growing increasingly indifferent and hostile to the Constitution's natural law philosophy. Certain jurists, using such ploys as legislating from the bench, showed a total contempt towards the tried and tested doctrine of *stare decisis*. It was the judicial activism of the Earl Warren Court (1954–1968) and to a greater extent, the Warren Burger Court (1959–1986), that radically perverted the original intent of the Framers and substituted the Constitution's original natural law jurisprudence with the sophistry of positive law as judges' primary vehicle in modern judicial decision making.

Religion generally, and Judeo-Christianity specifically, more than any other constitutional issue, has been the subject of the liberal activist courts wrath in its continuing efforts to separate law from morality. Beginning with *Everson v. Board of Education*,[1] the Court announced to a shocked American public its discovery of a new "constitutional" doctrine. Justice Frankfurter and his plurality had suddenly found in the First Amendment, "a great wall of separation between Church and State," that had heretofore alluded such great jurists as John Marshall, Joseph Story, Oliver Wendell Holmes, and Benjamin Cardozo. Thus, the positive law doctrine of the separability thesis, had achieved constitutional legitimacy by separating the Church—the foundation of all morality, and the State—the foundation of all legality. Armed with the judicially-created doctrine of separation of church and state, such radical liberal and anti-Christian organizations as the ACLU, People for the American Way, the National Education Association, atheists and agnostics and many other leftist special interest organizations openly hostile to America's Judeo/Christian heritage, with the help of the Supreme Court, began to systematically eradicate all vestiges of our historical, religious, and Christian practices in all public spheres—the main battle ground being the public schools.

In *Engel v. Vitale*,[2] the Court held that a verbal prayer offered in a school is unconstitutional, even if it is both voluntary and denominationally neutral. In *Stein v. Oshinsky*[3] and *Collins v. Chandler Unified School District*,[4] freedom of speech and press was guaranteed to students unless the topic was religious, at which time such speech becomes unconstitutional. In *Stone v. Graham*,[5] the Court held it is unconstitutional for the Ten Commandments to hang on the walls of a classroom "since the students might be lead to read them, meditate upon them, respect them, or obey them." Only a Court, holding great contempt to the original intent of the Framer's natural law philosophy in constitutional decision making, could have the hubris to contradict America's historical closeness of church/state relations in the judicial opinions mentioned above.

On the issue of profanity, the Court has likewise drastically changed its view held during the Framers time. In *Cohen v. California* the facts stated that:

> appellant was . . . wearing a jacket bearing the words "Fuck the Draft" in a corridor of the Los Angeles Courthouse. Held . . . the State may not . . . make the simple public display of this single four-letter expletive a[n] . . . offense. . . . The [California statute] infringed his rights to freedom of expression guaranteed by the First and Fourteenth Amendments of the Federal Constitution. . . . This is not . . . an obscenity case. . . . That the air may at times seem filled with verbal cacophony is, in this sense not a sign of weakness but of strength.[6]

This type of jurisprudence amounts to the deconstruction of over two hundred years of Court opinions that had little problem distinguishing between profanity and legitimate freedom of speech. For example, the Court held in *People v. Rug-*

gles,[7] where the Court condemned a book that referred to Jesus Christ as a "bastard," stated "[n]othing could be more offensive to the virtuous part of the community, or more injurious to the tender morals of the young, than to declare such profanity lawful . . . and shall we form an exception in these particulars to the rest of the civilized world?" Today this would be called censorship. However, the early Court took on an activist role in upholding the morality of the people, not in denigrating it, as today.

The Court also used positive law jurisprudence in *Erznoznik v. City of Jacksonville,*[8] when the city tried to forbid the showing of indecent movies in public drive-in theaters because the screen was visible from two adjacent public streets and a nearby church parking lot. The language of the statute was narrowly drawn and stated:

> It shall be unlawful . . . for any . . . drive-in theater in the City to exhibit . . . any motion picture . . . in which the human male or female bare buttocks, human female bare breasts, or human bare pubic areas are shown, it . . . visible from any public street or public place.[9]

The Court, under the guise of positive law, ruled this ordinance "[i]nvalid . . . [as] an infringement of First Amendment rights. . . . Nor can the ordinance be justified as an exercise of the [city] . . . for the protection of children."[10] In discussing a similar case, the Court of a century earlier evoked a strong natural law jurisprudence in its analysis in *The Commonwealth v. Sharpless,* the Court held:

> The destruction of morality renders the power of the government invalid. . . . The corruption of the public mind, in general, and debauching the manners of youth, in particular, by lewd and obscene pictures exhibited to view, must necessarily be at-

tended with the most injurious consequences. . . . No man is permitted to corrupt the morals of the people.[11]

In the area of blasphemy (taking God's name in vain), the Court's present day rulings are also antithetical to those of the Framer's generation. In *Grove v. Mead School District*,[12] the Court refused to remove the book, "A Learning Tree," that a high school sophomore was required to read for her literature class because of several outrageous passages like one, "Declaring Jesus Christ to be a poor white trash God, or a long-legged white son-of-a-bitch." This ruling once again differed markedly from the natural law jurisprudence in *Ruggles,* where a certain book said, "Jesus Christ was a bastard, and his mother must be a whore" [the Court held that] . . . "Such words . . . were an offense at common law. . . . It tends to corrupt the morals of the people, and to destroy good order. Such offenses . . . are treated as affecting the essential interests of civil society." [13]

The question of freedom of speech is likewise riddled with inconsistencies since positive law has become the dominant legal philosophy of the Court. One can now have free speech protection to use the word "God" in a derogatory manner as long as its hyphenated with other profanity. However, this constitutional protection stops when using God in a respectful manner in a public forum. For example, in the *State of Ohio v. Whisner,*[14] the Court held that, "To include reference to God . . . in State Board of Education minimum standards relating to operation of schools would violate the establishment clause of the First Amendment." This sentiment was further underscored in *Reed v. van Hoven*[15] where the Court held that, "During the regular school day . . . no themes will be assigned on such topics as, "Why I believe . . . in religious devotions." The Establishment Clause of the First Amendment has now been corrupted by modern jurists to mean that it is constitutional to show the most blasphemous contempt for God, while at the same time, unconstitutional to show any reverence or devotion toward God in the public schools. These absurd positive law rulings ring true the words of Abraham Lincoln—"The philosophy of the school room in one generation will be the philosophy of government in the next."[16]

Since the early 1900's, natural law has been steadily on the decline as the controlling philosophy in American legal jurisprudence until an unusual incident happened that catapulted it back onto the scene of the legal community. The incident concerned no trial, case, lawyer, or judge directly, but would later affect them all. What I am speaking of is Martin Luther King's, *Letter from Birmingham Jail*.[17] In this letter, King dramatically utilized Aquinas's natural law philosophy in demanding civil and political rights for Black Americans in the 1960's. In 1963, King and others were arrested in Birmingham, Alabama for unlawfully protesting against that city's *de jure* segregation laws. In his jail cell, on strips of toilet papper, King penned a passionately compelling defense of his protests against the scathing demonstrations by many White clergymen. King justified his breaking the "law" by appealing to a "higher law"—the natural law, and asks a seminal question—can we as God's creation, created in his image, for his glory, be under any obligation to obey laws that contravene God's immutable laws found in scripture? King's answer was emphatically NO! King argued further as Aquinas, Locke, and Blackstone had before him, that any laws of man that contradict God's immutable laws are void and cannot be law because such laws are immoral.

Contrasting with the natural law of Aquinas and King was law professor and legal theorist Lon Fuller, who wrote an essay criticizing Hart's positive law philosophy holding that, "law" and "what is morally right" are inseparable.[18] Central to Fuller's natural law analysis was a principle he called, "fidelity to law."

For example, Fuller stated that, "if, as I believe, it is a cardinal virtue of Professor Hart's argument that it brings into the dispute the issue of fidelity to law, its chief defect, if I may say so, lies in a failure to perceive and accept the implications that this enlargement of the frame of argument necessarily entails."[19] Fuller defined fidelity to law as a law, statute, or an ordinance as something deserving of loyalty and respect by its very existence of being law. Fuller then argued that unlawful regimes like the Nazi's are greatly misunderstood by positivists like Hart because they assume that there was something akin to "law" in Nazi Germany in the sense of fidelity to law, or a law that legitimately deserved respect and obedience. Therefore Fuller argued that positive law's inability to distinguish between Nazi "law" and "fidelity to law" makes the entire theory of positivism jurisprudence patently false.

Fuller recognized the existence of immoral rules, but says that such rules that are a part of a comprehensive legal system are profoundly evil and unjust. Fuller analyses the problem of restoring respect for law and justice after the collapse of the Nazi regime that respected neither. For example, Fuller cites the so-called "grudge-informer" case where a disgruntled wife, wishing to rid herself of her husband because of her infidelity with other men, falsely accused her husband of being a traitor to *der Fuhrer* by concocting a story that she heard him speak against Hitler and the Nazi party while home on furlough. The husband was imprisoned for a short while, but instead of being executed, he was sent to the front line. After the defeat of the Nazis, he brought his wife up on charges of false imprisonment. His wife defended that according to Nazi law, her husband's comments amounted to breaking the law. Fuller maintains that these so-called "grudge-informer" cases were not "law" because they failed to keep any semblance of legal order and that for any legal system to be legitimate, some degree of moral content in the law must be recognized—i.e., impartial enforcement, independent judiciary, fair notice, due process, a shared and predictable system of values. Fuller believed that law had its own "internal morality" or "good order" which positivism held that law only had to maintain "order." Hart, faced with this conundrum, was forced to recognize Nazi law, but then he would refuse to apply it, but Fuller countered that if law is fidelity to law then how can any court refuse to uphold it unless the laws were never valid in the first place? Fuller concludes that positive law is an inadequate legal theory for jurisprudence because it is utterly impotent to explain mankind's moral obligation to the fidelity of law.

American Legal Realism: Holmes and the "Bad Man"

In the early 1930's, a third school of legal theory emerged that sought to understand the law in the most concrete fashion possible. *Realists,* as they were known, believed that the legal theories of natural law and positive law were too cerebral and abstract to be relevant in modern jurisprudence. Realists like Oliver Wendell Holmes, Benjamin Cardozo, Roscoe Pound, and Karl Llewellyn began to look at explicitly what lawyers, judges, and the courts actually do as really being the law, and not what theorists like Blackstone and Austin say they should do. The realist rallying cry was "law in action" as opposed to "law in the books." Justice Oliver Wendell Holmes, in his celebrated essay, *The Path of Law,*[20] elucidated the core tenants of what later became known as legal realism. To understand realism, you must see this theory as an outgrowth of the times it came from—the industrial revolution—where the late nineteenth century saw perhaps the greatest growth of technology and science than all the previous millennia of mankind combined! How could the law keep pace with these innovations?

Holmes and others realists were actually reacting to an earlier legal movement called *formalism,* championed by C. C. Langdell, Williston, James Barr Ames, and others who in the late 1870's sought to combine the rigors of scientific empiricism to legal precepts. The result was the "casebook method" that applied the logic of deductive reasoning to studying the law by applying a pre-existing "rule of law" straightforwardly to the facts, thus determining the proper conclusion or holding of the Court. These "law as science" theorists became Holmes major target in his book, *The Path of Law,* when he stated that, "the life of the law has not been logic, it has been experience."

Holmes argued against a formalist approach to the law through the eyes of an archetypal person he calls the *bad man.*[21] This is supposed to be the average person whose only concern is the end result, the bottom line or how much can I get away with before the law punishes me? For example, Holmes's *bad man* views a contract not as a moral obligation or in normative terms as "keeping one's word," but simply as a choice between competing obligations—perform the contract or pay the penalty. Likewise in tort law, Holmes's *bad man* would view the theory of paying damages for a negligent act he afflicted on someone as nothing more than a tax—the State is punishing me for my negligent act. Therefore, Holmes concludes that a proper understanding of law is closer to the art of *predicting* rather than *deducing.* How much I can get away with before society punishes me versus using logical deduction to reach a specific conclusion. Holmes and the realist movement insisted that there is no logic in the law as the formalists maintained, but held that in actual practice, judges and the courts do not use logic to decide cases in the sense of using the "rule of law" in deducing from general legal principles to specific conclusions. Holmes saw no logic in the law because he believed that the law developed very slowly based on the traditions and history of the people abiding under such laws. This fact Holmes felt formalism failed to understand, for he saw law not as a fixed canon of immutable commandments, but law as a constantly shifting, "evolving" set of rules that accommodate themselves to the constantly changing demands and interests of society. Law historians, Dornan and Vedlik, quoting Holmes' relativist approach in judicial decision making, stated that, "[t]he belief that truth cannot be immutable, that there are no abiding, timeless truths or absolute moral norms, because reality is judged to be in a constant state of flux. 'Truth'. . . is whatever works in a given situation."[22] This is classic positive law jurisprudence that most modern jurists use in their judicial decision making. Historian John Eidsmoe outlined several precepts of this relativistic philosophy as applied to law:

1. There are no objective, God-given standards of law, or if there are, they are irrelevant to the modern legal system.
2. Since God is not the author of law, the author of law must be man; it is law simply because the highest human authority, the state, has said it is law and is able to back it up.
3. Since man and society evolve, law must evolve as well.
4. Judges, through their decisions, guide the evolution of law.
5. To study law, get at the original sources of law—the decisions of judges; hence most law schools today use the "case law" method of teaching law."[23]

Holmes has remarked in an article he wrote in 1920:

Everyone instinctively recognizes that in these days the justification of a law for us cannot be found in the fact that our fathers always have followed it. It must be found in some help which the law brings toward reaching a social end.[24]

Some forty-three years later Holmes, still holding to the same legal positive dogma, stated in his seminal work, *The Common Law:*

> The felt necessities of the time, the prevalent moral and political theories, . . . even the prejudices which judges share with their fellow-men have had a good deal more to do than the syllogism in determining the rules by which men should be governed.[25]

Justice Holmes, writing for the majority in, *Trop v. Dulles,* held that "[the Constitution] must draw it's meaning from the evolving standard of decency that marks the progress of a maturing society".[26] Likewise, Cardozo, a no less equally revered jurist as Holmes, stated in his book, *The Nature of the Judicial Process,* that "I take judge-made law as one of the existing realities of life."[27] Dornan and Vedlik in a similar vein said, [the Court has] "Liberated itself from what the Declaration of Independence called "the Laws of Nature and of Nature's God."[28] Finally, it was Chief Justice Hughes who most succintly defined judicial activism by exclaiming, "The Constitution is what the judges say it is."[29]

Rationalization and Rule Skepticism

Notwithstanding Holmes and other realists' contempt for logic, deductive reasoning is exactly how judges and the courts come to decide cases and settle disputes—deducing conclusions from a preexisting "rule of law." The realist counters that the "rule of law" is nothing but subjective rationalization judges and the courts use to justify their opinions. Legal realist Jerome Frank has stated that the intrinsic quality of legal reasoning is an end/means paradigm. The judge, in deciding a case, looks to the end he wishes to achieve, or his "gut feeling," and crafts the necessary means via application of a "rule of law" to rationalize such a conclusion.[30] Another precept of realism follows a reasoning-as-rationalization approach to the law is rule-skepticism, holds that "the law . . . consists of decisions, not of rules."[31] Thus, realists have concluded that since judge's decisions are the law, the common law doctrine of *stare decisis* is no longer relevant in jurisprudence.[32] To the realist, the law was too much in a state of flux and indeterminacy for *stare decisis* to apply. Also, realists questioned the rationale of binding a judge's opinion in one case to a decision in another case decided many years before, because the judge in the latter case could always find some "distinguishing" fact from the earlier to justify having a different result since no two cases are exactly alike.

Realists are primarily concerned with the law, but also with judges, for it was in their hands ultimately what the law will or will not be. Holmes has remarked that, "the prophecies of what the courts will do in fact, and nothing more pretentious are what I mean by the law," and the "Law . . . as to any given situation is either . . . actual law, i.e., a guess as to a specific future decision." To this end, realists propose the study of judicial behavior (the sociology of law) holding that to understand the law, you must analyze the patterns of decisions a judge makes so that you can more accurately "predict" how a judge will rule on a particular position in a future case.[33] Two recent examples highlighted the importance of a judge's jurisprudence of the past, present, and especially possible future opinions in the nomination to the Supreme Court of Judge Robert Bork,[34] which tragically failed for purely political reasons, and Judge Clarence Thomas, whose nomination barely passed Senate confirmation. The central questions of both nominees concerned their past decisions on such controversial topics as right of privacy, abortion, natural law, civil rights, affirmative action, substantive and procedural due process, judicial review, as indications of how they would likely decide cases if selected to the Supreme Court.

Conclusion

Classical man understood all law to be derived from God. The presumption was that, "God's word was to be obeyed." Natural law was based on moral principles (i.e., laws against theft, perjury, adultery, etc. . . .). However, during the late nineteenth and early twentieth centuries, certain legal theorists, lawyers, judges, philosophers, scientists, and other intellectuals said that these laws no longer have any connection to the metaphysical realm. In place of laws based on Judeo-Christianity came laws of the utilitarian—law that provided the greatest good for the most people, or did the least harm to the smallest number of people. Law was now stripped of any theistic devotion and became purely consequential and used primarily to maintain social order and achieve secular, humanistic ends. However, positive law soon encountered many internal contradictions. For example, how can a system of laws that seeks to maintain social order ignore moral concerns? Certainly no social order is achievable if people don't value moral order and the inalienable rights of all people—life, liberty, property. The sophistry of *Law as law* doctrine, as history has repeatedly shown, can only lead to genocide, despotism, and anarchy. However, natural law is the only legal philosophy that puts no trust in man. Natural law realizes that since Adam, mankind has been in a fallen state of nature and to have any hope of a successful human government, his foible propensities must be subjugated to the immutable principles of God. History has shown us repeatedly and even today, that to do otherwise, tyranny will prevail. That is why the Framers of the

Constitution incorporated the doctrine of separation of powers. The colonists were well aware from their experiences with England that a concentration of too much power in one branch of government was the enemy of liberty and of the people. It is clear that from all source materials of the period that natural law was the only philosophy that our Constitution was based on. All of the most important books, pamphlets, and Court decisions at that time conclusively prove this. Positive law, legal realism, Critical Legal Studies, and their parallel philosophies in the literary field—naturalism and cultural relativism, have proven themselves wholly inept legal philosophies for maintaining the rule of law.

Notes

1. *Everson v. Board of Education*, 330 U.S. 1, 18 (1947).
2. *Engel v. Vitale*, 370 U.S. 421 (1962).
3. *Stein v. Oshinsky*, 48 F.2d 999 (2nd Cir. 1965), *cert. denied*, 382 U.S. 957.
4. *Collins, v. Unified School District*, 644 F.2d 759 (9th Cir. 1981), *cert. denied*, 454 U.S. 863.
5. *Stone v. Graham*, 449 U.S. 39 (1980).
6. *Cohen v. California*, 403 U.S. 15, 18, 20, 25, (1971).
7. *People v. Ruggles*, 8 Johns 545, 547 (Sup. Ct. N.Y. 1811).
8. *Erznoznik v. City of Jacksonville*, 422 U.S. 205, 207 (1975).
9. Ibid., pp. 206–7.
10. Ibid., p. 205.
11. *The Commonwealth v. Sharpless*, 2. Serg. & R. 91, 103, 104 (Sup. Ct. Penn. 1815).
12. *Grove v. Mead School District*, 753 F. 2d 1528, 1540 (9th Cir. 1985), *cert. denied*, 474 U.S. 826.
13. *Ruggles*, pp. 545–546.
14. *State of Ohio v. Whisner*, 361 N.E. 2d 750 (Sup. Ct. Ohio 1976).
15. *Reed v. Van Hoven*, 37 F. Supp. 48, 56 (W.D. Mich. 1965).
16. Stephen McDowell and Mark A. Beliles, *America's Providential History*, Providence Press, Charlottesville, VA, 1989, p. 95.
17. Cited by David Adams, *Philosophical Problems in the Law*, Wadsworth Publishing Company, Belmont, CA, 1992, pp. 59–62.

18. Lon Fuller, "Positivism," *Harvard Law Review,* 71 (1958), p. 630.
19. Ibid., p. 632; See also Ibid., pp. 652–55.
20. Oliver Wendell Holmes, "The Path of Law," *Harvard Law Review,* 10, (1897), p. 45.
21. Cited by Adams, *Philosophical Problems,* pp. 91–92.
22. See Robert K. Dornan and Csaba Vedlik, Jr., *Judicial Supremacy, The Supreme Court on Trial,* Plymouth Rock Foundation, MA, 1986, p. 70, "The belief that truth cannot be immutable, that there are no abiding, timeless truths or absolute moral norms, because reality is judged to be in a constant state of flux. Truth . . . is whatever works in a given situation."
23. Cited by David Barton, *The Myth of Separation: What Is the Correct Relationship Between Church and State?,* WallBuilder Press, Aledo, TX, 1992, p. 203.
24. Cited by ibid., p. 204.
25. Cited by ibid., p. 204.
26. *Trop v. Dulles,* 356 U.S. 86, 101 (1958), Cited by Barton, *What Is the Correct Relationship Between Church and State?,* p. 204.
27. Benjamin Cardozo, *The Nature of the Judicial Process,* Yale University Press, New Haven, CT, 1921, p. 10.
28. Dornan and Vedlik, *Judicial Supremacy,* p. xi, "[the Court has] Liberated itself from what the Declaration of Independence called "the Laws of Nature and of Nature's God." Finally, it was Chief Justice Hughes who boldly exclaimed that—"The Constitution is what the judges say it is." Cited by Barton, p. 204.
29. Cited by Barton, p. 205.
30. Jerome Frank, *Law and the Modern Mind,* Anchor Books/Doubleday, NY, 1963, p. 50.
31. Ibid.
32. Steven Burton, *An Introduction to Law and Legal Reasoning,* Little, Brown, Boston, 1987, pp. 1, 19–39, 41–43, 68–73, 76–77; Joseph Hutcheson, "The Judgment Intuitive," *Cornell Law Quarterly,* 14, (1929), pp. 274–88.
33. Ibid.
34. Judge Robert Bork poignantly chronicles the process of his failed nomination to the Supreme Court in his book, *The Tempting of America: The Political Seduction of the Law,* Free Press, NY, 1990, pp. 271–322.

7
Seeking to Separate the Inseparable
The Myth of Separation: What Is the Correct Relationship between Church and State by David Barton

November 1996

David Barton in his book, *The Myth of Separation*, exposes the long held "constitutional" doctrine—separation of church and state, for the pure sophistry it is, lacking any constitutional foundation. In this book, Mr. Barton has extended into the 1990's what authors like—Dornan and Vedlik's book, *Judicial Supremacy* (1986); Daniel L. Driesbach's, *Real Threat or Mere Shadow: Religious Liberty and the First Amendment*, and John Eidsmoe's seminal work, *Christianity and the Constitution (1987)*, did in the late 1980's by rendering a thoughtful and throughly researched critique of liberal constitutionalism, revealing the true origins of American Constitutional law, the men that influenced and wrote it, and the controlling philosophy behind it. David Barton's tome has greatly contributed to the burgeoning movement in constitutional law scholarship that has been going on since the early 1980s, offering a prudent and well-reasoned alternative approach to the secular revisionist view of constitutional law in concisely chronicling what the Framers of the Constitution and the early Courts actually said and believed—using their own words and not what others said they believed when drafting America's founding documents—the Declaration of Independence, the Constitution, and the Bill of Rights.

The Myth of Separation is a comprehensive and thoroughly revealing historical analysis of the origin of the controversial phrase, "separation of Church and State." Barton shows us how this doctrine found its way into the landmark Supreme Court decision, *Everson v. Board of Education*,[1] by which Justice Frankfurter, writing for the majority held, "[the] First Amendment has erected a wall between church and state. That wall must be kept high and impregnable. We could not approve the slightest breach." The eighteen chapters embellish and develop this theme under the following headings: The Way It Is; The Way It Was—Building the Constitution and The First Amendment: The Origin of the Phrase "Separation of Church and State"; The Court's Early Rulings—We Are a Christian Nation; Other "Organic Utterances;" Protection from the Absurd: The Absurd Becomes Reality; The Absurd Becomes the Standard; The Court's Definition of Its Position; Dilemmas for the Court?; Double Standards; Toward A New Constitution? Even A Child, . . . " . . . Government of the People By the People, For the People; . . . ." Judicial Supremacy—The Potential Downfall of the Republic; The Solution. Barton's treatment is straight forward and easy to read. Most revealing, however, is that the history he uncovers is so antithetical to what most law, political science, and history students are taught, as to make one at first incredulous and then profoundly disappointed that the jurists, historians, teachers, and the guardians of our American heritage have so thoroughly corrupted the Constitution as to make it totally opposite of what was the Framer's original intent.

This book provides an amazing amount of historical information about the Founders, their beliefs for a sound government, and the philosophy behind the drafting of the Constitution.

Barton delineates the background of our founding documents as well as the strategic and tactical considerations that existed prior to the drafting of the Constitution which continued to be respected, in Supreme Court judicial opinions well into the late 1940's. The author has done a tremendous amount of original research and has cited copious amounts of primary sources to support his primary contention that the Founders all believed in God, and most openly professed Christianity, and that these Christian views were expressly transmitted into our founding documents, state constitutions, local laws, ordinances, statutes and in early judicial opinions.

Section Three (The Origin of the Phrase "Separation of Church and State") (pp. 41–46) states that neither this doctrine nor the phrase are found in either the Constitution, nor in the First Amendment or the Bill of Rights, but was first coined by Thomas Jefferson in a letter to a group of Connecticut ministers from the Danbury Baptist Association. These ministers had written President Jefferson to voice their concerns and fears of a state-sponsored church similar to the Anglican Church of England. This sentiment had previously been addressed by the Framers of the Constitution twelve years before in the very first statement of the First Amendment: "Congress shall make no law respecting an establishment of religion nor prohibit the free exercise thereof." However, the ministers from Danbury wanted more assurance, so on January 1, 1802, President Jefferson responded to their letter, expressly stating:

> The federal government would not establish any single denomination of Christianity as the national denomination. I contemplate with solemn reverence that act of the whole American people which declared that their legislature should "make no law respecting an establishment of religion, or prohibiting the

free exercise thereof, thus building a wall of separation between Church and State."[2]

Barton states that "wall" was a unilateral one and was understood by Jefferson, the Framers, and the Courts as keeping the government out of the church and not as it is used in today's jurisprudence, to purge all influence of the church (i.e., Christianity) from the state or in any state sponsored, public forum, particularly the public schools. Barton reasons that two primary philosophies have led to the decline of constitutionalism in U.S. Constitutional law—*Relativism* and *Legal Positivism,* leaving modern day judges and lawmakers without the original natural law philosophy that the Framers and the early Courts used to create and to interpret the Constitution. And, although the Framers' natural law ideas concerning limited government, separation of powers, and respect for individual liberty was the primary jurisprudence until the late 1940's. Since that time, natural law has gradually and systematically fallen out of favor and is virtually a dead letter in the minds of most jurists today. Consequently, when a ruling needs to be made on the moral issues of the day—abortion, euthanasia, the death penalty, pornography on the Internet, Church/State relations, etc.—modern jurists and decision makers are without a fixed body of controlling principles upon which to aid them as they seek solutions to the myriad of societal and moral ills. Barton argues that this lack of an underlying body of immutable principles translates into the arbitrary constitutional adjudication we have today.

Barton's work is not just a book on constitutional law, but is a fascinating and comprehensive compendium of primary sources of pre-constitutional philosophers like—Aristotle, Aquinas, Grotius, Pufendorf, Richard Hooker, Hobbes, Locke, and Montesquieu; contemporary philosophers, theologians, and statesmen like Blackstone, Franklin, Hamilton, Jefferson,

Madison, and Mason; and post-constitutional thinkers like John Marshall, Joseph Story, John Witherspoon, Noah Webster, and Patrick Henry, all held together with Barton's terse and non-ostentatious commentary style. Barton discloses an astounding piece of research on the source materials used by the Framers in writing America's founding documents (p. 195). This monumental study was done by two political science professors—Donald S. Lutz and Charles S. Hyneman, which included their review of a total of 15,000 items including 2,200 books, newspaper articles, pamphlets, and monographs of political materials written between 1760-1805. From this material, Lutz and Hyneman discovered that the three philosophers quoted more frequently by the Framers than any others were—Baron Charles Montesquieu, Sir William Blackstone, and John Locke,[3] and that all three men were strong natural law adherents. Equally astonishing was another source quoted four times more frequently than Montesquieu or Blackstone, and twelve times more frequently than Locke—the Bible. According to Lutz and Hyneman, "the Bible accounted for 34% of all the founders' verbatim quotes. Another 60% of their quotes were drawn from authors who had derived their ideas from the Bible, thus, 94% of all the writings that influenced the Framers of the Constitution were either directly or indirectly attributable to the Bible!" This is an astounding fact, because constitutionalism, especially since the 1940s, was primarily influenced by positive law, which is the diametrical philosophy opposite the philosophy of natural law—positive law holding to the belief of the separation of law from morality, while natural law views law and morality as inseparable.

Barton, throughout his book, cites case law (mostly Supreme Court decisions) to support and augment his primary thesis that America was a Christian nation established on natural law precepts (p. 201). To this end, Barton extends much space to chronicling the origins of modern day positive law—namely relativism, or as applied through the courts, legal positivism (p. 203). Barton states that the philosophy of positive law holds the following tenants:

1. There are no objective, God-given standards of law, or if there are, they are irrelevant to the modern legal system.
2. Since God is not the author of law, the author of law must be man; it is law simply because the highest human authority, the state, has said it is law and is able to back it up.
3. Since man and society evolve, law must evolve as well.
4. Judges, through their decisions, guide the evolution of law.
5. To study law, get at the original sources of law—the decisions of judges; hence most law schools today use the "case law" method of teaching law.

To prove how pervasive legal positivism has become in modern judicial decision making, Barton cites the views on this topic by such noted jurists as Oliver Wendell Holmes,[4] Benjamin Cardozo,[5] Earl Warren,[6] Warren Burger,[7] Evan Hughes,[8] and Harvard law Dean Roscoe Pound, as all being strong adherents to the philosophy of relativism and positive law jurisprudence in interpreting the Constitution (p. 204). Barton argues that the Constitution is best interpreted through the original natural law philosophy of the Framers in American law. For Barton, these basic ideas are self-evident and should replace the relativist doctrine of legal positivism as the only legitimate form of constitutional jurisprudence. To this end, Barton presents many landmark Supreme Court opinions of old and prophetic utterances of the founders, philosophers, theologians, and statesmen who influenced these early judicial opinions. He does so in a coherent and intelligent manner, highlighting and expounding upon examples of natural law principles that occurred throughout American history and

American constitutional law which are, he argues, most suited to governance and law in dealing with a growing multitude of contemporary problems and societal decay.

Barton's primary thesis is not only that modern Supreme Court Justices have greatly disparaged the original intent of the Framers, but having destroyed the Constitution's original natural philosophy that undergirded it and gave the Constitution meaning, cannot agree on a set of fundamental principles of constitutional interpretation. By comparing the Framers' contemporary writings, intent, and early judicial opinions against current decision making on the Court, Barton clearly delineates the markedly different holdings on virtually identical issues, and indicates how the doctrine of original intent has been held in the highest contempt by many of today's decision makers, and shows by analogy, how much societal moral standards have been debased by the Court's holdings. Barton compares and contrasts modern and original judicial opinions regarding such moral issues as profanity, lewdness and indecency, blasphemy, religious belief, atheism, and Sunday laws (pp. 179–186). For example, on lewdness and indecency, Barton cites *Erznoznik v. City of Jacksonville*,[9] where a city ordinance to prohibit public drive-in theaters from showing indecent movies which were visible from two public streets and a church was struck down by the Court as, "an unconstitutional infringement of First Amendment rights. . . . Nor can the ordinance be justified as an exercise of the [city] . . . for the protection of children." However, in the *Commonwealth v. Sharpless* decision, the Court ruled on a similar case in an earlier era:

> The destruction of morality renders the power of the government invalid. . . . The corruption of the public mind, in general, and debauching the manners of youth, in particular, by lewd and obscene pictures exhibited to view, must necessarily be at-

tended with the most injurious consequences. . . . No man is permitted to corrupt the morals of the people.[10]

In analyzing these judicial opinions on a legally similar statute, I find it difficult to determine how the Court in 1815 can find a sound constitutional reason to protect our youth from indecency without a violation of freedom of speech being considered by the jurists and fail to find the same constitutional principle in 1975? The reason, Barton contends, is the controlling philosophy jurists used to help them reach their decision. In 1815, the philosophy jurists used in constitutional decision making was *natural law;* by 1975, it was *positive law.* In Barton's view, the proper response to this doctrinal confusion is to abandon the modern-day positive law jurisprudence (which has caused our present-day "constitutional crisis") and replace it with the jurisprudence the Framers originally intended to guide our understanding of the Constitution—that being the philosophy of natural law. Barton argues:

> Advocates of natural law believe, as did the Founders, that there are fixed standards for right and wrong. Proponents of relativism believe that the only thing absolutely wrong is having fixed standards of right and wrong. Those who resent restraints and discipline proclaim, "You can't legislate morality!"

"That is not true. Relativists fail to realize that morality is always legislated—it is simply a matter of whose morality is being legislated" (p. 252). Any legitimate constitutionally sound jurisprudence, Barton argues, must include the substantive concerns of the drafters of the first amendment, modified as necessary to be responsive to the problems of modern society. The conflicts involved in the first amendment adjudication can best be remedied by applying natural law principles because these principles, expressly provided for in the Bill of Rights, were a purposeful and substantive attempt by the Framers to address future conflicts between the Executive, Legislative, and Judicial branches.

Barton's solution to our "constitutional crisis" isn't to rewrite first amendment law by identifying specific rules of decision. Rather, he seeks to remove the wrong information from constitutional decision making (legal positivism), replace it with correct information (natural law), and then to act on this new information. Facing the general criticism that natural law lacks a comprehensive, coherent philosophical underpinning because of it's normative principles, Barton responds that, "morality is vital to the success and prosperity of both nations and individuals," (p. 255). And:

> Civil law can address only externalized crimes, but Christianity, however, can address and help prevent crimes while they are still internalized. In the case of murder, Christianity can deal with it before it occurs; the civil laws can do nothing until after the fact. Civil laws do not deal with the heart, which is the actual source of violence, crime, drug abuse, etc. . . . Without the aid from religion, government utilizes extensive manpower and expends massive sums attempting to restrain behavior which is the external manifestation of internal sins. The moral teachings of Christianity provide a basis for civil stability which allows a government to perform its primary function: serving, not restraining (p. 253).

Barton elucidates upon the normative concepts in natural law by restating it as the right, for individuals to govern themselves under God. The fundamental meaning, however, is that the Founders were well aware from history and personal experience, that state repression of public morality leads to a lack of respect for Christianity and eventually to societal denigration. This was why the colonies insisted upon including a Bill of Rights before a majority of states (9 of 13) would agree to ratify the Constitution as the law of the land. Note that the first ten amendments to the Constitution (the Bill of Rights) are expressly addressed to Congress—"Congress shall make no law. . . . ." is the constant refrain. The genius of the Framers was in that they so worded the Bill of Rights as to give explicit protection to the inalienable rights of the people against the Leviathan government. Finally, it should be mentioned at this point that the Declaration of Independence, the Constitution, and the Bill of Rights are all natural law documents, conspicuously based on Biblical Christianity and theistic principles.

This natural law view is based on a social contract between the people and government—the consent of the governed. These principles were incorporated throughout all of the political institutions created by the Framers. In Barton's view, "the phrase, the 'law of nature,' not only was a key term identifying the natural law philosophy, it was a very revealing term in our founding documents" (p. 197). Barton responds to the dangers of legal positivism used by the majority of today's judges as being "derived from the philosophy of relativism (later called pragmatism), which had been promoted by the American philosophers Charles S. Pierce, William James, and John Dewey" [11](p. 201). The natural law view imposes numerous limits on majority rule in favor of minority interests. Clearly, Barton favors these limits for the same reason as James Madison did, to prevent the "tyranny of the majority," which is the political end in a pure democracy where the majority vote always rules. In a similar vein, Barton argues that America was not conceived by the Founders to be a strict democracy, but a republic. He cites Benjamin Franklin's famous statement when addressed by a lady shortly after the first Constitutional Convention—the lady asked, "well, Dr. Franklin, what have you done for us?" Franklin responded, "My dear lady, we have given you a Republic—if you can keep it" (p. 229). In a Republic, there is a built-in presupposition that legality and morality are synonymous. In a pure Democracy, no such law/moral dichotomy exists. The majority rules whether the issue is slavery, euthanasia, legalizing drugs, or abortion.

Perhaps the author's most compelling point is that our society has inherited natural law as the foundation of our constitutional system, and that all other political and philosophical positions are inherently alien and inferior to it. He reflects how the Framers, like all other governments in history, had a particular political philosophy that guided them in their formation of their new Republic. Summing up the Framers' search for an adequate philosophy for their Constitution, Barton quotes the speech Franklin gave at the first Constitutional Convention (p. 195). "We have gone back to ancient history for models of Government, and examined the different forms of those Republics which having been formed. . . . And we have viewed Modern States all around Europe." Barton states that, "the philosophers embraced by the Founders all expounded a similar theme: the importance of natural law and the Bible as the foundation for any government established by men. Natural law and the Bible formed the heart of our Founders' political theories, and was incorporated as part of their new government." In place of legal positivism, Barton offers his natural law view, historically rooted and constitutionally legitimate. While the practicality of his approach is not easily established by empirical evidence, the theory itself provided a strong theoretical foundation for the world's oldest continuing democracy. As such, viewed by most scholars today, natural law is at worst provocative and at best, an interesting, but archaic philosophy of little relevance in current law or judicial decision making. Why has natural law lost its preeminent position as the guiding philosophy in constitutional interpretation? Some scholars believe that perhaps it never really occupied this position. Others hold that natural law is merely a time-bound ideology inadequate to meet present day problems faced by the Court. Barton suggests that:

> It required decades for the Supreme Court to dispose of natural law. Gradually relativism discarded God from public affairs, and redistributed governmental powers among the branches. These actions were slow, but steady, gradual, but systematic. Therefore, correcting what has happened in and to America will not necessarily occur within a single year or through a singular act. (p. 257)

Barton's contention is that just as natural law was gradually removed from constitutional decision making, so must it gradually be replaced back to it's rightful position in order to remedy our present constitutional crisis.

Natural law was particularly susceptible to both political and ideological challenges for several reasons. First, Barton points out the arguments used by early natural law philosophers to demonstrate the superiority of their ideology, such as appeals to higher law, natural rights, self-evident truths. The evidence here is consistent and compelling. Montesquieu, for example, believed, "The Christian religion, which ordains that men should love each other, would, without doubt, have every nation blest with the best civil, the best political laws; because these, next to this religion, are the greatest good that these men can give and receive."[12] Blackstone, likewise holding to his strong natural law beliefs, held that, "Man, considered as a creature, must necessarily be subject to the laws of his creator, for he is entirely a dependent being. . . . And consequently, as man depends absolutely upon his maker for everything, it is necessary that he should in all points conform to his maker's will. This will of his maker is called the law of nature."[13] Philosopher John Locke said that, the "Law of Nature stands as an eternal rule to all men, legislators as well as others. The rules that they make for other men's action, must . . . be conformable to the Law of Nature, i.e., to the will of God . . . no human sanction can be good, or valid against it."[14] Additionally, the author notes that substantial inherent contradictions existed between the main goals of legal positivism—that all law is subjective; that man is the author of all law; that law, man, and society must evolve together; and, that judges are the final arbiters of what the law is. It would appear that even early legal positivists could not agree on how to promote one goal without interfering with another. For example, legal positivists have always grappled with the problem of majority rule and minority rights. Natural law recognizes both, although the two philosophies frequently clash. However, with the Bible as the foundational document of the Constitution, and natural law as its controlling philosophy, such human aberrations as slavery, racism, and *de jure* discrimination, though unjustly given constitutional sanction in America by the Founders, in time had to fall if we were to maintain this Republic. This is true because one of the Biblical premises undergirding the Constitution is that, "We the people" are all "created" in the image of God, and to "love thy neighbor as thyself." These foundational Christian principles are found throughout America's founding documents, including the Constitution, and was a mortal blow to the many Machiavellian tendencies of the White slave holders toward *their* Black brothers from 1619–1865. For example, slavery in America was given legal sanction and flourished for over 250 years because the majority of voters (land-owning White men at least 21 years old), in 1789, deemed that slavery would be given constitutional legitimacy. However, although slavery was preserved in the Constitution, since the Constitution was a natural law document with a strong Biblical, anti-slavery underpinning, that "peculiar institution" was doomed to extinction as people began to realize that Black people also were human, created in the image of God, to be accorded certain "inalienable rights among these, life, liberty, and the pursuit of happiness." Unfortunately, it took a bloody civil war to end slavery, but because of the moral, natural law-based crusades of the abolitionist and free-thinking northern liberals in the Republican party, by 1865, slavery was given its death blow in America. Would applying a positive law philosophy to the Constitution have resulted in the end of slavery? I think not because positive law recognizes no moral authority other than raw sovereign power. Positive law respects no appeals to a metaphysical deity. This inability to rationally mediate conflicts between morality and law is one of positive law's central inadequacies in serving as a viable philosophy in constitutional decision making. Barton offers the natural law view as a solution to this problem, and maybe it is. But, as the author concedes, this theory is far from being recognized as a viable jurisprudence in contemporary constitutionalism.

One of the many virtues of this work, in particular, is that it is historically rigorous, and it's arguments are unimpeachably sound. Rather than conceive of a wholly original theory on how to interpret the Constitution, of which the literature is presently under deluge, Barton rediscovers the original natural law doctrine of the Framers. It is difficult to think of a more appropriate starting place when considering an interpretive model for constitutional decision making. Barton's discussion of natural law doctrine is, however, very accessible for the layman, student, and scholar alike. The book maintains a cohesive and smooth flow from chapter to chapter. This is true despite the fact that the author's natural law doctrine is not expounded upon in detail until chapter 12, and then only after the basic natural law historical perspectives are presented and contrasted with rival political and philosophical ideologies. Any confusion this approach engenders, however, does not detract from the book's ultimate usefulness because Barton's analysis of the ideas of the Framers and their contemporaries, as well as the fate of the natural law doctrine after the *Everson* decision, is as interesting as it is necessary to the development of his perspective on reintroducing normative, natural law philosophic principles back into constitutional decision making.

In conclusion, it would be helpful for the reader to have a prior acquaintance with the works of the legal philosophers and theorists Barton critiques. Nevertheless, *The Myth of Separation* offers an excellent theoretical and practical apologetic to some of legal positivist's most sacred cows. That it does so in a particularly careful and thoughtful way increases the likelihood that it may contribute to a return to our Framers' original intent of constitutional jurisprudence.

Notes

1. *Everson v. Board of Education,* 330 U.S. 1 (1947). *An excerpt of this chapter was published in *The Social Critic,* November– December, 1996, pp. 36–7.
2. Henry S. Commager, ed., *Documents of American History,* Appleton-Century-Crofts, Inc., NY, 1948, p. 179.
3. John Eidsmoe, *Christianity and the Constitution,* Baker Book House, MI, 1897, pp. 51–3.
4. Barton quotes Justice Holmes as openly rejecting the beliefs of the Framers when he stated, "Every one instinctively recognizes that in these days the justification of a law for us cannot be found in the fact that our fathers always have followed it. It must be found in some help which the law brings toward reaching a social end." See Oliver Wendell Holmes, "The Law in Science—Science in Law," in Collected Legal Papers, Harcourt, Brace and Co., NY, 1920, p. 225, in David Barton, *The Myth of Separation: What Is the Correct Relationship between Church and State?,* WallBuilder Press, Aledo, TX, 1992.
5. Barton said of Cardozo that "Justice Cardozo, as a strong relativist, also rejected fixed standards and rights and wrongs." Barton quotes Cardozo as writing that "If there is any law which is back of the sovereignty of the state, and superior thereto, it is not law in such a sense as to concern the judge or lawyer, however much it concerns the

statesman or moralist. See Benjamin Cardozo, *The Growth of the Law*, Yale University Press, 1924, p. 49; cited by Barton, *The Myth of Separation*, p. 204.

6. "Chief Justice Earl Warren, who served on the Court from 1953–1969, wrote about the Constitution in *Trop v. Dulles*, 356 U.S. 86, 101 (1958), explaining that the Constitution: "Must draw its meaning from the evolving standards of decency that mark the progress of a maturing society (p. 204).

7. Chief Justice Burger was the author of the Court's opinion in *Lemon v. Kurtzman*, 403 U.S. 602 (1971) outlining a three-part test for establishment clause cases that amounted to a removal of anything having the remotest religious significance as unconstitutional if held in a public setting or supported by public funds.

   As a general rule, the Court has developed a three-pronged test to determine whether a statue (or government action) violates the Establishment Clause:

   a. The statue must have a secular purpose.

   b. Its primary effect or purpose must neither advance nor inhibit religion.

   c. The statute must not foster excessive entanglement between church and state. See *PMBR Multistate Workbook*, Multi-State Legal Studies, Inc. Santa Monica, CA, Vol. 1, Constitutional Law Section, 1995, p. 26.

8. Chief Justice Charles Evan Hughes said: "The Constitution is what the judges say it is." Evan Corwin, *The Constitution and What it Means Today*, Princeton University Press, NJ, 1937, p. xxiv.

9. *Erznoznik v. City of Jacksonville*, 422 U.S. 205, 207 (1975).

10. *Commonwealth v. Sharpless*, 2 Serg. & R. 91, 103, 104 (Supreme Court of Penn.) (1815).

11. The belief that truth cannot be immutable, that there are no abiding, timeless truths or absolute moral norms, because reality is judged to be in a constant state of flux. "Truth" . . . is whatever "works" in a given situation. See Ronald K. Dornan and Csaba Vedlik, Jr., *Judicial Supremacy: The Supreme Court on Trial*, Plymouth Rock Foundation Press, MA, 1986, p. 10.

12. Charles Montesquieu, *The Spirit of the Laws*, Isaiah Thomas, Worcester, Vol. I, 1802, pp. 125–126.

13. William Blackstone, *Commentaries on the Laws of England*, Clarendon Press, Oxford, 1771, Vol. I, p. 39.

14. John Locke, *The Second Treatise on Civil Government*, Prometheus Books, NY, 1986, p. 75.

8
Speaking Coherently, Honestly, and Freely about Race: *The End of Racism* by Dinesh D'Souza
Racism Mythology vs. Black Pathology

February 24, 1997

Part 1: Racism Mythology

Every one hundred years or so, there arises a person who thinks and writes so clearly, logically, and with such sublime moral authority, that the very truth of his words sends the charlatans and hypocrites of that age scrambling for cover like vermin fleeing the sight of light in a dark, dank alleyway. This person has the unique ability to say what he means and back it up with copious, authoritative facts; to herald the truth, even if he alienates some of his ideological comrades who may still find some of the conclusions of his thesis personally affronting and difficult to accept, not because his thesis isn't true, but what the implications of his findings might be to their cherished icons, if they are! On this point, G. K. Chesterton and C. S. Lewis come to mind.

Dinesh D'Souza, on the surface would be an unlikely candidate to be this man-of-our-time. A man who in his book, *The End of Racism,* has shaken the intellectual foundations of our beliefs and taboos about racism, its origins and development in eighteenth-century Europe, and how it differs from related and often confused with such terms as *discrimination* and *prejudice*. Mr. D'Souza is neither Black, (which would grant him almost instant credibility in many liberal circles of academia and in the civil rights community) nor is he a White liberal, which although he would be less credible and "authentic" to some in the Black community (by his very race), the liberal establishment as a whole would be rather sympathetic to his views. Dinesh D'Souza is an Indian (born in India) who was converted to Catholicism as a child and immigrated to America with his family where he received his formal education, graduating from Dartmouth University in 1983. Presently, he is the John H. Olin Scholar at the American Heritage Institute and the author of the *New York Times* bestseller, *Illiberal Education* (1991).

Although Mr. D'Souza is neither White nor Black, yet he speaks very passionately and with dauntless authority on the volatile issues of race which have plagued America since its founding. He writes from a point of view not often heard from (Indian/immigrant), and you hear from him none of the hackneyed cliches on race that the liberal and conservative theorists unstintingly hold to as dogma. However, D'Souza isn't purely ideological nor iconoclastic, but writes with a two-edge sword, shredding many commonly believed but erroneous assumptions about race, getting to the ultimate issue of the race question—personal responsibility. D'Souza holds that the major problems facing the Black people in America are not racism, discrimination, and poverty, as pundits on both sides contend, but "promiscuity, ignorance, and crime."

I have divided this review essay into two parts to conform to the book's basic division whereby D'Souza compares and contrasts two dominate themes: Part I: *Racism Mythology* (pp. 2–3), explores the most commonly held (but false) beliefs most people have about racism; and Part II: *Black Pathology* (pp. 6–7), chronicles the multitude of destructive aberrant tendencies afflicting the Black community, economically, socially, culturally, physically, and spiritually. I have used his headings as an outline for this book review. D'Souza brilliantly outlines, refutes, and/or bolsters the many conflicting and contradictory philosophies about race, dispelling the various mythologies about racism and exposing the real problems of African Americans which he thoroughly chronicles throughout the book as: *ignorance, crime, and promiscuity.* It is my contention that if such pathologies had happened to a nation, that country would have long declared a state of emergency and marshaled all of its resources to remedy the problem, much like the systematic way America, through the Marshall Plan, rebuilt Germany and Japan after World War II.

In the book, *The End of Racism,* D'Souza painstakingly traces the philosophical origins of modern-day liberalism and the social policies it spawned in American society over the past sixty years, beginning with the nineteenth-century philosophy of relativism and its various antecedents in academia—Social Darwinism, in science, Modernism in art, dance, and music, Legal Positivism in law, and Cultural Relativism in the humanities, the latter term serving as the primary focus of this book review. D'Souza cites anthropologist and Columbia University professor Franz Boas as being the arbiter and disseminator of the philosophy of cultural relativism in the American academy during the late nineteenth and early twentieth century, and through his work and the work of his many famous pupils—Margaret Mead, Ruth Benedict, Otto Klineberg, Kenneth Clark, Melville Herskovits, Theodosius Dobzhansky, Alfred Kroeber, Robert Lowie, Edward Sapir, L. C. Dunn, Isidor Chein, Gene Weltfish, and Ashley Montagu, thrughly shaped our present-day thinking not only about race and racism, but every branch of the academy including law, philosophy, the humanities, and science.

Franz Boas was of Jewish and German extraction who immigrated to America in 1886 due to the menace of anti-Semitism sweeping Europe in the late nineteenth century. It was in America where he served as Chairman of the Anthropology Department at Columbia and as the founder of the American Anthropological Association, that served as a platform in further developing his ideas on using cultural relativism—the belief that all cultures are equal, in his attack against Social Darwinism—the belief that different levels of civilizational standards can be attributed to various levels of evolutionary development among the races. D'Souza says of Boas and the new generation of scholars he influenced that:

> they adopted a relativist position: standards are in the eye of the beholder, so that Western criteria should not be used to evaluate non-Western cultures . . . all cultures are equal . . . non-Western cultures were morally superior to Western civilization, because they were closer to nature (p. 142).

Racism Mythology #1

Racism is simply an irrational prejudice, a product of ignorance and fear

This popular belief about racism implies several erroneous ideas: (1) "[R]acism is universal, a universal staple of the human condition; (2) Racism always existed in the West; (3) Racism manifests itself in the English language in terms like "blackmail" and "black sheep." D'Souza wastes little time in attacking this common myth about racism, which he defines as "an ideology of intellectual or moral superiority based upon the biological characteristics of race" (p. 27). The classical liberal understanding of racism is that it is an irrational product of ignorance and fear. This sounds plausible on the surface, but its implications are untenable. History has shown us that racism was basically invented in the West and was a rationally conceived, well-thought-out philosophy rooted in the humanistic, scientific theories of the Enlightenment Period. For liberals to causally dismiss racism as simply a product of ignorance and fear shows us that they neither understand the scientific, historical, and philosophical roots of racism, nor do liberals offer any viable remedies to combating it—for if one doesn't understand a problem, it is very unlikely that he will discover the proper solution. Such has been America's woefully inadequate legacy in dealing with race. Racism was not founded by American Whites and nurtured at Ku Klux Klan rallies in the back woods of Southern towns in the nineteenth-century Mississippi or Alabama, but racism was formulated in the ivory towers of academia of Western Europe's most prestigious universities of the eighteenth and nineteenth centuries—Berlin, Bonn, Vienna, Munich, Paris, Rome, London, Madrid, and stamped with the imprimatur of scientific legitimacy. D'Souza contends:

> Although it [racism] can be found in embryonic form among the Chinese and the Arabs in the late Middle Ages, racism is a modern and Western ideology . . . developed in Europe as a product of the Enlightenment, part of a rational and scientific project to understand the world. For European travelers, missionaries, and ethnologists, racism provided a coherent account of large civilizational differences that could not be attributed to climate and were thus considered intrinsic. Racism originated as a theory of Western civilizational superiority (p. 27).

Racism Mythology #2

Slavery was a racist institution, and the Constitution's compromise with slavery discredits the American founding as racist and morally corrupt

This is one of the more inflammatory and enduring myths that D'Souza skillfully refutes. His premise being that if slavery was a racist institution, then practically all races and nations are racist because at one time or another, all races practiced slavery in some form. D'Souza writes:

> Slavery was practiced for thousands of years in virtually all societies: in China, India, Europe, the Arab world, sub-Saharan Africa, and the Americas. In the United States, slave owning was not confined to whites: American Indians and free blacks owned thousands of slaves. Thus slavery is neither distinctively Western nor racist. What is uniquely Western is the abolition of slavery. The American founders articulated principles of equality and consent which formed the basis for emancipation and the civil rights movement (p. 22).

Slavery is morally reprehensible and dehumanizing because it treats our brother as an animal. It is true that some of America's founding fathers practiced slavery. They were wrong and should be justly criticized for owning slaves and for giving the institution of slavery constitutional legitimacy, but that is only half the story. In reading about the hundreds of debates the Framers had on this subject and the intense and equally vocal support to end slavery by many White Americans, including many of the signatory's of the Constitution, one cannot in all honesty contend that **all** White people supported slavery. Other examples of anti-slavery events in American history include the

Abolitionist movement, the many Whites who risked their lives helping slaves escape to freedom in the North, the death of an old political party, mired in the past (the Whigs) and the birth and success of a new political party founded on the abolition of slavery (the Republicans), all should be given more weight by the detractors of the founding fathers. Also, in America, a civil war was fought over the very issue of slavery where "five whites died for every slave." Add to that, the Reconstruction period, the civil rights movement, which reached and reformed the highest branches of our executive, judicial and legislative government, culminating in the passage of the Civil Rights Act (1965) and the Voting Rights Act (1964). D'Souza writes:

> Not only was slavery extensively practiced in the ancient world, . . . but in the modern era slavery was prevalent in Africa, the slave trade was actively promoted by the Arabs, American Indians owned slaves, and there were even thousands of black slave owners in America (p. 71). In this sense, neither America nor it's Founders were any more morally corrupt than the rest of the world at that time.

Today, in America, racism, where it is found is dealt with in a very punitive and drastic way. However, America's (and by analogy the West's) approach to eradicating slavery is markedly different than non-Western countries of which the abolition of slavery was a non-issue. I challenge the reader to find any non-Western country with any history whatsoever of fighting to end slavery in their country to any degree. You won't find any examples because in most non-Western societies, no semblance of democracy existed. On this issue, D'Souza writes: "In most parts of the world, slavery was uncontroversial for the simple reason that the concept of freedom simply did not exist." Orlando Patterson writes, "Indeed there was no word for freedom in most non-Western languages before contact with western peoples" (p. 71).

Racism Mythology #3

Segregation was as system established by white racists for the purpose of oppressing blacks

Combating this myth about racism, D'Souza writes:

> Segregation developed not as an expression of this radical racism but in response to it: it represented a compromise on the part of the Southern ruling elite seeking, in part, to protect blacks. Despite the limited world which segregation imposed, blacks maintained intact families, voluntary associations, and cohesive communities. Escaping to Midwestern and Northern cities, many blacks created a rich culture of learning, art, and music, reaching its pinnacle in the Harlem Renaissance (p. 170).

Here, I must disagree with D'Souza's premise that segregation was neither an expression, nor a response to radical racism, but simply a continuation of what preceded it. Under slavery, Blacks and Whites often lived and worked on the same plantation, however, they lived starkly contrasted and segregated lives. In general, Whites enjoyed the best of life that they could afford, while Blacks were relegated to animal-like existence and treatment. D'Souza offers a unique and inconspicuous historical paradox about how segregation ended:

> Who fought segregation? Not the liberals: there were few outspoken liberals in the South and their opinions were irrelevant. Rather, it was the private companies such as streetcar owners

who mounted the only significant, albeit unsuccessful, opposition. This private sector resistance is explained by the fact that segregation in the government does not impose a severe burden on public agencies, which are monopolies. . . . By contrast, private companies found that segregation raised their costs and inconvenience of doing business, and raised the specter of reduced demand for those goods and services. . . . Segregation, therefore, represented a triumph of government regulation over the free market (p. 180).

Here also, I must disagree with D'Souza's premise that segregation "represented a compromise . . . to protect blacks." On the contrary, history shows no such benign view of *de jure* segregation as practiced in America. For example, after the Civil War, an ambitious project called Reconstruction was set in motion to help Black people achieve equality under the law and to afford them full constitutional rights. To this end were the Thirteenth, Fourteenth, Fifteenth Amendments to the Constitution ratified by Congress which ended slavery, made Black people American citizens, and afforded Black people the right to vote. However, as the nineteenth century drew to a close, the Federal government caved in to political pressure (largely from the South) to jettison Reconstruction, which did occur and on the ash heap of broken promises and failed dreams of Black people, arose a systematic campaign of racial terrorism against Blacks by groups like the Ku Klux Klan, and institutional structures like the black codes, *de jure* segregation, and making a spectator sport out of lynching Black men (and women) without a trial, for no reason, or for a contrived, trivial infraction.

Racism Mythology #4

In American history, racism is the theory and discrimination is the practice

Liberal dogma in this area holds, "Racism is based on ignorance. Ignorance generates prejudices and stereotypes. Such predispositions lead to irrational fear. Fear produces hate. Hate produces discrimination" (p. 116). D'Souza's analysis of the three historical models of racism unveils some interesting facts. The models are: (1) The *barbarism/civilization model;* (2) The *evolutionary (biological) model;* and (3) The *cultural relativism model.* D'Souza writes:

> The earlier understanding was based on a distinction between barbarism and civilization, and on an evolutionary model in which biological groups called races were seen to occupy ascending places in a hierarchy. The new paradigm is based on cultural relativism, which in this cultures are equal. According to this now-entrenched view, no group may be considered superior or inferior, group differences are largely the product of environment and specifically of unjust discrimination, all attempts to attribute intrinsic qualities to groups reflect ignorance and hatred, so that the mission of sound policy is not to civilize the barbarians, but to fight racism and discrimination (p. 117).

In general one, could say the classical view of race from the beginning of time to Darwin (1860s) followed the barbarism/civilization model. From Darwin to about the 1940s, followed the evolutionary model, and from the 1940s to modern times, social scientists have primarily used a cultural relativism model to explain cultural differences. However the cultural relativism model has many or more problems than the politically incorrect prior two models. First of all, the cultural relativism model lumps all races together as equal and ignores obvious intellectual disparities and levels of civilizational standards among the races of the world. To attribute these differences to "environment," "unjust discrimination," "fear, ignorance and hatred," ignores many examples of Blacks who under more dire circumstances than that faced by any Black person in America today, yet succeeded to levels above that of most White Americans of their day. Secondly, cultural relativism doesn't explain why newly arrived immigrants from all over the world can come to America with little money, education, or a command of the English language, and in less than a generation, start their own successful businesses, and send their children to America's top Ivy League universities. This achievement of the American dream isn't relegated to immigrants from Asian countries, but immigrants of African descent from the Caribbean Islands, South America, and all countries of Africa. On the average, most other racial groups are doing much better economically and are better integrated socially than many American-born Blacks whose families have been in America for generations. Therefore, it is ludicrous to continue to attribute Black failure to the theory of racism and its so-called practice of discrimination in America, all other races and nationalities of the world (including African) continue to prosper in America's free-market democracy.

Are all forms of discrimination illegal or morally indefensible? Most liberals would immediately say yes because of their adherence to the philosophy of cultural relativism. However, if one looks at that question logically and objectively, you must come to the conclusion that not all forms of discrimination are bad, and that you as an individual discriminate in a variety of circumstances many, many times every day. For example, on a superficial level, today I am wearing a white shirt and black pants. At home I have a closet with other colored shirts and pants, but on this day I discriminated against all other shirts and pants in favor of the ones I am wearing now. Is that bad? No! Yet, I discriminated. On a more substantive note, pick any decision that you have made at anytime in your life on any issue and think of the infinite number of choices you could have made differently. D'Souza writes:

> Evidence for the old discrimination has declined, but there are many indications that black cultural pathology has contributed to a new form of discrimination: rational discrimination. High crime rates of young black males, for example, make taxi drivers more reluctant to pick them up, storekeepers more likely to follow them in stores, and employers less willing to hire them. Rational discrimination is based on accurate group generalizations that may nevertheless be unfair to particular members of a group.(p. 24)

Whatever choices you make in life, you discriminated against an infinite number of other possible choices, whether it was choosing a spouse, car, house, hairstyle, presidential candidate, movie rental, etc. By necessity, we must discriminate. This is rational discrimination and makes common sense. The question then becomes, should society allow illegal discrimination regarding people's fundamental rights? Of course not.

Racism Mythology #5

The civil rights movement represented a triumph of justice and enlightenment over the forces of Southern racism and hate

This myth about racism is often spoken of using the metaphors of Biblical figures: Moses leading the children of Israel out of the bondage of slavery in Egypt, or David vs. Goliath.

The way the metaphors are used is that the civil rights movement (and those who agree with its philosophical aims) are Moses or David, and all other people of a different opinion as being the Pharaohs and Goliaths of the world—racist, hateful, in dire need of re-education. However, this scenario has several problems. D'Souza states:

> [T]he civil rights movement imploded because of confusions and contradictions within its own basic principles. Heroes appear less heroic when it turns out that they have only a limited understanding of the nature of their struggle. Yet in order for us to understand where the civil rights movement may have gone wrong, it is essential to question its premises, and to ask whether they were misconceived from the start (p.169).

In separating reality from rhetoric, D'Souza's analyses of the historical and philosophical origins of the civil rights movement by showing its direct ideological roots to cultural relativism. D'Souza writes, "History shows that the principles of the civil rights movement developed as a direct outgrowth of cultural relativism. The guiding assumption was that racism is the theory and segregation and discrimination are the practice" (p.169).

Few people would argue that *de jure* segregation and discrimination are morally wrong. However, the civil rights movement insistence on cultural relativism as its guiding ideology failed to adequately understand why segregation was necessary—to protect Blacks from physical annihilation from Southern Whites who were hostile and bitter over loosing the Civil War and their cherished quality of life. D'Souza writes:

> It was right to oppose segregation, but it misconstrued both the purpose and effects of segregation. It correctly targeted discrimination, but wrongly construed private individuals and companies, rather than government, as the primary threat to

black prospects. . . . It harbored, from the outset, an expectation of group equality that would eventually prove destructive to its own cherished principle of nondiscrimination (p.169).

History shows that in the hundred year period from 1865–1965, the end of Slavery and the Civil War, through the flowering of the civil rights movement, the Black family, under dreadful and oppressive circumstances, maintained its unity. However, beginning in the early 1960s, as segregation and *de jure* discrimination was being dismantled, ironically, began the erosion of the stable two-parent Black family which had for so long provided a familial safety net, protecting Blacks during their darkest hours in America. The civil rights movement, because of their unilateral focus on white racism, has all but ignored anti-social and pathological character deficiencies among their own people. The results of this neglect has been a tragedy of Biblical proportions as Black pathologies soar to new heights.

Racism Mythology #6

Although Martin Luther King, Jr. helped to secure formal rights for blacks, white racism has become more subtle and continues its baleful influence throughout institutional structures

One of the most damning indictments against Martin Luther King, Jr. and the civil rights movement was its inability to be totally intellectually honest with itself, their constituency, and White America. The rhetoric of the civil rights movement was always strong when confronting White racism. This was right to do, for racism and discrimination was (and to a lesser degree) still is, a barrier to African Americans entering the mainstream of society, but civil rights activists seem to turn a blind eye to the myriad of other barriers to Black success in American society, namely Black pathology, which was becoming increasing evident by the late 1960s. D'Souza writes:

> Why did white liberals and black activists abandon color blindness as a basis for law and policy? The civil rights movement in which both groups participated embodied from the outset the assumptions of cultural relativism: the presumed equality of all cultures or groups. Martin Luther King, Jr. emphasized one serious problem faced by blacks (racial discrimination) while ignoring another equally serious one (cultural deficiencies), which inhibited black competitiveness. Thus, equal rights for blacks could not and did not produce equality of results. Consequently, many liberals and civil rights activists invoked equality of results to prove that white racism continues unabated. They supported affirmative action and racial preferences in order to fight the effects of past and present racism. (p. 22)

The ever-widening gulf among Blacks between the middle and upper class and the underclass are not because of White racism, whether institutional or otherwise. This is the red herring liberal civil rights activists like to focus on to take the spotlight off of a once successful, but now woefully failed movement that has lost its moral compass. Black activists, by frequently, aggressively, and systematically "playing the race card," and overrelying on aberrant racial incidences like the beating of Rodney King by White policemen caught on video tape, the Bernard Goetz vigilante shootings on a New York subway, and the O. J. Simpson criminal and civil trials, to galvanize the Black masses, have instead left them empty, frustrated and angry. This spurious strategy has only obscured the true issues causing many Blacks to fail to see any need to better themselves by themselves. I am referring to the old Horatio Alger "can-do" philosophy of pulling one's self up by your own bootstraps when one is beset by life's many challenges and difficulties. This was the pattern American Blacks followed in the past as their forefathers had done as slaves and during the Reconstruction and post-Reconstruction eras. This explains the ambivalence and contempt civil rights organizations and Blacks nation-wide showed toward self-help remedies when Justice Clarence Thomas suggested at his confirmation hearing that "pulling himself up by his bootstraps" was exactly what he did to gain entrance into a prestigious Catholic prep-school, Yale Law School, and eventually to become only the second Black person to sit on the U.S. Supreme Court. Unfortunately, practically all of the Black liberal civil rights organizations actively fought against his nomination simply because Justice Thomas rejected a cultural relativist ideology that fostered Black dependance on governmental largess as a legitimate means to help Blacks succeed. Justice Thomas, through his writings, speeches and the life he lives, urges Black people to seek after hard work, moral uprightness, personal discipline, and self-help remedies, to better their lot in life.

To many liberal activists, racism has now gotten so bad in America that it has taken on a personal quality all its own. No longer is it the overt racism of a Bull Connor or a Governor Wallace blocking the path of Black students seeking to desegregate a high school in Little Rock, Arkansas, or admission to the University of Mississippi, but when racial disparities in society are discovered, Black activists cry, INSTITUTIONAL RACISM!!!—the implication being that racism is so ingrained in American society that it permeates all of its institutional structures. Under this paradigm, it is impossible to fight racism (if indeed, that's what it is). Racism has now gone underground. Racism is as invisible and pervasive as the air we breathe. On this point D'Souza comments:

> Traditionally, racism refers to an ideology of biological superiority. The concept of institutional racism abandons this conventional view, divorcing racism from the concept of intentions or even individuals who are alleged to hold racist views. For the first time, racism is regarded as an impersonal force, an invisible hand, which operates through the structures of society to thwart black aspirations. One may say that the accusation of institutional racism infers the presence of racism from the failure of existing rules and standards to produce equality of results between racial groups. The persistence of inequality generates a conviction of imposed inferiority (pp. 290–291).

Liberal activists know that the philosophical underpinnings of their ideology are flawed and wholly untenable, but the stakes of power brokering are high, and as long as they can frame the debate in the increasingly irrelevant terminology of White vs. Black; Rich vs. Poor; Haves vs. Have Nots, instead of focusing on the true dichotomies in society: Hard working vs. Lazy; Smart vs. Ignorant; Dependant vs. Independent; Promiscuous vs. Moral; Victim vs. Victimizers, the plight of Black people will not improve. However, using the latter type of language has moral implications and demands individual and personal accountability to validate their attendant measurable consequences. In our present-day debate about race, it is liberals alone who are the sole prognosticators regarding race and racism. It is they alone who can find, identify, and rectify racism wherever it is (or isn't), using American tax dollars to fund failed program after failed program. D'Souza writes:

> Since racism is an ideology of biological superiority, "institutional racism" is a nonsense phrase that avoids the real problem, which is that even under the same rules, all groups do not compete equally well. Liberals seem to be hopelessly divided between a commitment to procedural justice—which is the essence of liberalism—and a desire to rig the rules in order to foreordain the results. The consequence is to weaken the

moral foundation of liberalism itself, which ceases to be a just arbiter of competing claims and becomes one redistribution vision among many. It is time for genuine liberals to abandon the destructive ideology of "institutional racism" and to rediscover the virtues of merit and standards evenly applied (pp. 335-336).

Finally, on this issue D'Souza details an insightful comparative analysis of the two principal philosophical approaches that Blacks historically have used in combating race and racism in America. The two traditional schools of thought on this subject are of Booker T. Washington and W. E. B. Dubois. I have outlined some of D'Souza's primary contentions on these two men and put them in chart form to emphasize their markedly different approaches. One seeks to remedy Black failure through self-improvement of the whole man, the other seeks redress of civil rights because of White racism.

Booker T. Washington	W. E .B. Du Bois
Acknowledged Black cultural and character deficiencies and provided practical and specific remedies.	Emphasized White racism and encouraged Blacks to fight for their civil rights via the judicial process.
Legacy = University Development, i.e., Tuskegee Institute— to improve Black people intellectually, socially, and morally.	No legacy of university development. Legacy = civil rights/activist institutions (NAACP; SCLC; Black Urban League, etc.)
Self-Help, pull yourself up by your bootstraps approach for economic success in America.	Litigate-Litigate-Litigate for your constitutional rights, Affirmative Action, Quotas.
Prove racists to be wrong through hard work, moral uprightness, and academic achievement.	Black people's problems stem primarily from White Racism. De-emphasizes personal responsibility or self-help remedies.
Controlling philosophy— Biblical theism. If a man won't work, a man should not eat.	Controlling philosophy—cultural relativism. Because I am a human being, I deserve a certain standard of living, whether I work for it or not.

Racism Mythology #7

The civil rights leadership is committed to fighting racism and building up the economic and cultural strengths of blacks, especially the poorest ones

Ironically, the last thing civil rights activists want is the end of racism because this would put them out of a job and severely curtail their public influence on racial issues. So Black activists fan the flames of every racial incidence (White against Black, of course), wherever it may be found and even if race isn't directly evident, it can be easily invented via the vehicle of "institutional racism." If the civil rights leadership was so committed to ending racism in America, why do you see them fight against any rational remedy to enlighten their constituency or to substantively improve the lives of Black people? For example, Truth in Sentencing legislation; School choice; Private School Vouchers for the poor; "Ending welfare as we know it," and requiring recipients to work for "their" benefits, putting a time limit of two years for welfare recipients to become totally self-sufficient, etc., have all faced vehement opposition from civil rights activists, for they know that when the poor and underclass realize that they don't need the race merchants anymore, and that they can make it out of poverty on their own through hard work, the charade that liberals actually "care" for the poor and that racism is the reason that they are poor, will be over. D'Souza notes:

> While the underclass cannot rely on the civil rights establishment, however, the civil rights establishment does rely on the black underclass. This is the dirty little secret of the race merchants. As Glenn Loury writes, "the suffering of the poorest blacks creates a fund of political capital upon which all mem-

bers of the group can draw when pressing racially based claims." Not only this, but as the National Research Council reports, "A large proportion of lower-status blacks receive public assistance and community services from programs that are disproportionately staffed by black professionals." The point is that the civil rights establishment has a vested interest in the continuation of black poverty. What E. Franklin Frazier wrote of the black bourgeoisie in the 1950's is even more true of the civil rights establishment: "The lip service which they give to solidarity with the masses very often disguises their exploitation of the masses" (p. 241).

You have heard the old saying that "politics makes strange bedfellows." Well, when the civil rights activists forsook the color-blind philosophy of King for the seduction of racial classifications and preferences, they got in the bed with the very people that they, by definition, were opposed to; namely White Supremacists, Neo-Nazis, KKK, Aryan Nation, and various other racist, segregationist groups. D'Souza writes:

> To achieve equality of result, an expectation generated by the relativist premise that all groups are inherently equal, civil rights activists with the support of many white liberals began to abandon their long-standing commitment to color blindness, and although no doubt with nobler motives, to imitate the racists and segregationists by putting racial classifications and racial preferences back into the law. (p. 215)

The civil rights movement no longer has any legitimacy, its moral authority and the African American constituency they supposedly serve, sacrificed on the altar of political expediency and governmental largess.

Racism Mythology #8

Affirmative action is a policy that assures equal opportunity for disadvantaged African Americans and other minorities

D'Souza quotes Justice Harry Blackmun on affirmative action—"In order to get beyond racism, we must first take account of race. In order to treat some persons equally, we must treat them differently" (p. 215). D'Souza further writes:

> The contemporary debate over affirmative action is a kind of idiots' quarrel between those who chant the word "goals" and those who whisper the word "quotas." Liberals and civil rights activists form the first group: we only want goals. Conservatives dominate the second group: you really want quotas. Yet quotas are simply goals reified. Are they wrong because they rigidly endorse goals or because they unfairly discriminate in the first place? (p. 215)

In theory, affirmative action was to provide a "level playing field" whereby Blacks and other minority groups could compete for jobs and educational opportunities. But when the civil rights leadership forsook the color-blind philosophy of King, affirmative action no longer had any relationship to finding the best candidate for the job, but became a racial numbers game that was an unofficial measure of determining whether an employer had the correct number of minorities at his company. To have too few minorities at your company became synonymous with practicing racial discrimination in the work place and subjecting one's self and your company to a multitude of lawsuits and a relentless barrage of negative press by the civil rights activist's willing accomplices in the media, regardless of the viability of such claims of discrimination.

For the past thirty years or so, affirmative action programs have been the Achilles heel of the civil rights movement in the public relations area, as these groups grope toward being relevant in an increasingly merit-based society. D'Souza writes:

> The practical issue was: how to quickly and substantially increase the number of blacks in schools and jobs? Both the ideology of cultural relativism as well as the more immediate prospect of continued social unrest compelled a liberal change of policy. The consequence of this change was that Martin Luther King's vision of a color-blind system of laws and policies was destined to enjoy a very short and precarious life in American law. Gradually but indisputably, affirmative action metamorphosed from a project to recruit the best person for the job into a program to prefer minority applicants with weaker credentials over better qualified white applicants who are turned away. The color-blind path became the road not taken. (p. 220)

Having forsook Dr. King's objective, merit-based approach to ending racism and improving the socio-economic lot of Blacks and other disadvantaged minorities, liberal activists took the low road and offered White America threats of a "long, hot summer" if draconian and present changes in employment practices weren't immediately implemented. The unfortunate outgrowth of this legislation became the numbers game we have today. That's why Jesse Jackson and his group, Operation PUSH, can go to a company like Texaco, or megapublisher, R.R. Donnelly, and state that because they lack a visible number of minorities in their work force, notably in upper management positions, that immediate and systematic changes must be implemented including minority management-track programs and mandatory racial sensitivity classes for all its employees. Large multi-million and multibillion dollar corporations, fearing civil rights law suits and unflattering media exposure, cave in to such demands, while affirmative action's original intent that the issue of race play an increasingly lesser role, and true merit play the primary role in choosing candidates for employment or entry in higher educational institutions, has been forgotten. In our present-day racially bewildered climate, true and substantive affirmative action, based solely on merit, has become a dream deferred.

Racism Mythology #9

Multiculturalism unites Blacks and non-White immigrants in a common struggle against White racism

Afrocentrism is the theory, Multiculturalism is the practice. Black activists, in their struggle against White racism, have substituted racism and discrimination with their own unique brand of exclusionary and equally immoral twin ideologies—*Afrocentrism* and *Multiculturalism*. Afrocentrism seeks to view history, politics, religion, and all forms of knowledge as having originated in Africa, and, because of historical revisionism by White racist professors and historians, Africa's rightful place in history and their contributions to civilizations were systematically marginalized and wrongfully accredited to other races and nations. Afrocentrism seeks to set the record straight, so to speak, and to accurately delineate Africa (and her progeny) their proper role throughout history. D'Souza writes:

> Many observers have been frustrated and bewildered by the controversy generated by Afrocentrism and Multiculturalism. Critics, including myself, have charged activists with sponsor-

ing distortions and excesses. Advocates insist that they seek nothing more than to correct historical biases and open doors and windows to the world beyond the West. For liberals who recognize that more is at stake than a mere outbreak of global curiosity, Multiculturalism and Afrocentrism have proved problematic yet impossible to completely jettison. (p. 338)

However, many of the central claims of Afrocentrists, like the ancient Egyptians were a Black race, or that the ancient philosophy of the Greek and Roman civilizations were stolen from philosophers in Black Africa, are wholly untenable and without any historical support. However, these "facts" are widely held as the Gospel by Afrocentrists and by many educated African Americans.

Multiculturalism seeks to view all races as equal despite the obvious substandard performances of some races, in practically every category of intelligence and mental development. Liberal activists, rather than addressing such disparities honestly, attribute them to White racism or charge that Whites are unfairly judging minorities by Eurocentric standards. But this is precisely what Afrocentrists and Multiculturalists seek to do by viewing world history through the ahistorical, rose-colored lens of Afrocentrism. D'Souza writes:

> The reason is that, whatever their abuses, Multiculturalism and Afrocentrism are logical outgrowths of the Boasian ideology of relativism. Cultural relativism dictates that since all cultures are equal, the relatively poor performance of some groups must be due to the fact that they are being unfairly judged by another group's cultural standards. Relativism also requires that differences of wealth and civilizational achievement cannot be explained by cultural superiority; rather, such differences must be due to the fact that the more powerful culture is oppressing others. Eurocentrism, in this view, is the racist system which explains why whites score higher than blacks on tests, and why

Western civilization is richer and more powerful than the Third World (p. 338).

Afrocentrism and Multiculturalism may be interesting ideologies to many, but they, like liberalism and cultural relativism, are woefully impotent to explain or offer any substantive remedies to the myriad of Black pathologies plaguing the Black community in America today.

Racism Mythology #10

Blacks and other persons of color cannot be racist because racism requires not just prejudice but also power

This myth became popularized by rapper, Sister Souljah's comments made during the 1991 Presidential debates between George Bush and Bill Clinton. However, this myth, like the previous nine, have glaring inconsistencies. D'Souza writes:

> Many liberals find it difficult to recognize Black racism because they are ideologically committed to view it as a mere reaction to White racism. In fact, African American racism is a **coherent** ideology of Black supremacy, promoted in Afrocentric courses and institutionally embodied in the Nation of Islam. In an increasingly meritocratic society, black racism becomes a rationalization for Black failure. Thus African American antagonism is most vehemently directed against groups such as Jews and Asian Americans that have no history of persecuting Blacks but that out compete them. (p. 23)

If racism is a one way street (Whites victimizing Blacks), as most liberal activists would contend, then explaining away examples of Black racism towards Whites as being impossible, or justify it as a legitimate reaction to White racism, has several problems: First of all, you don't need power to think racist thoughts, or even to act on them. Power simply limits the extent, opportunity, and effect of one's ability to affect others. For example, take the poorest, most powerless Black or Hispanic resident during the rioting in South Central Los Angeles because of their dissatisfaction with the Rodney King verdict, where several of the police officers that beat King (caught on video tape) were later freed after their first trial. I contend that these people are just as racist as the White CEO of a Fortune 500 company who uses racially discriminatory hiring practices at his firm to keep minorities in menial positions or not hire them at all, though they are qualified for better jobs . The only difference between the two is the *extent* and *scope* that each has to affect others.

When Black people act in a racist manner towards Whites, most liberals readily excuse such behavior as merely a reaction to White racism. This view is in line with their philosophy of cultural relativism—all races are the same and any differences can be attributed to culture and education. However, this rationalization, although superficially plausible, is basically paternalistic. White liberals are saying that Black people don't even have the intellect, power, or economic where-with-all to be racist. So like a permissive parent to a child in dire need of discipline through "tough love," Whites look the other way while Black racism increases. Ironically, this is the same phenomenon that occurred during the post-Reconstruction period of the 1880s. However, at that time, it was the backlash of White racism and resentment because of the meager economic and political gains Black people made during the Reconstruction period of the 1870s. D'Souza writes:

Why do many white liberals acquiesce in such sentiment? Because their ideology of relativism compels them to see black racism as nothing more than a reaction to white racism. Black racism is "the hate that hate produced," as a famous Mike Wallace documentary on the Nation of Islam put it. In this view, Blacks are historical victims and Whites are historical victimizers. Obviously victimizers do not deserve to be treated with respect: therefore so-called black racism is an understandable and partly legitimate response to the injuries of White racism. Thus, the argument goes, "White racism" is really a redundancy and Black racism, if it exists, is nothing more than an epiphenomenon of White racism. These assumptions, in varying degrees, are embedded in our public thought and discussion about race. They are reflected in countless news articles, essays and books about the relations between Blacks and Whites, and they are the foundation for many laws and policies, such as hate speech codes and antidiscrimination statutes which may be neutrally worded, but in practice, often focus on White offenders (pp. 406–407).

Racism Mythology #11

Racism is the main obstacle facing African Americans today and the primary explanation for Black problems

This is probably the most popular and most widely held explanation of Black failure by liberal activists—White racism. However, this myth is loosing much of its holding power, as an increasing number of Blacks from every socio-economic category honestly determine for themselves what are truly Black American's primary obstacles to success—It's not White racism, but Black pathology. D'Souza writes:

> The main contemporary obstacle facing African Americans is neither White racism, as many liberals claim, nor Black genetic deficiency, as Charles Murray and others imply. Rather it involves destructive and pathological cultural patterns of behavior: excessive reliance on government, conspiratorial paranoia about racism, a resistance to academic achievement as "acting White," a celebration of the criminal and outlaw as authentically Black, and the normalization of illegitimacy and dependency. These group patterns arose as a response to past oppression, but they are now dysfunctional and must be modified.(p. 24)

Blacks need to honestly determine who the enemy is. Most liberal politicians (Black and White) are trying to keep as many Blacks on the public dole as long as possible so as to foster irresponsibility and child-like dependance on federal handouts. This is accomplished while at the same time solidifying their 65-year monopoly on the political power base in the Black community. (It is not an accident that Blacks have voted for a democratic President in the 90 percentile since Franklin Delano Roosevelt's New Deal platforms of the 1930s.) Also, Whites aren't responsible for the cottage industry in the Black community of racist conspiracy theories against Black people perpetrated against them by Whites—from doctors intentionally inflicting Blacks with the AIDS virus, to a criminal justice system systematically and unjustly warehousing Black men in its prisons, purposely exacerbating the breakdown of the Black family. Is it the fault of White people that there is a strong and aggressive threat against academic achievement in the Black community to such an extent that in predominantly Black classrooms in public schools throughout America, high achieving Black kids are constantly under assault, harassed, and physically threatened by their poor-achieving peers for "acting White" or being a "wigger" (i.e., a Black person serious about academic success, or a Black person who [in the eyes of his peers] behaves like a White person).

Finally, D'Souza states that it isn't racism that keeps Blacks from getting ahead in society, but the deification of what D'Souza calls, the "*Bad Nigger*" archetype—a little discussed, but troubling phenomenon in the Black community. A Bad Nigger is a person who doesn't care about anything or anybody, who delights in criminal activity and resists any authority. (More about this role model in Black Pathology #10.) Far from the racism mythology of liberal activists is one of the most devastating pathologies afflicting the Black community—the bastardization of an entire race. In America, 65% of all Black babies are born out of wedlock, and in some cities, it is more than 80%! These and many other pathologies have been eroding the Black community since the 1960s while liberals and civil rights activists seem unwilling and certainly unable to provide moral leadership to stem the tide. Part II of this review essay addresses this and eleven other Black pathologies which are decimating many African American communities throughout America. D'Souza clearly outlines these problems in his book and offers blunt, but effective, and fresh solutions to old afflictions.

9
Part 2: Black Pathology

Black Pathology #1

The annual income of African Americans who are employed in full-time jobs amounts to about 60 percent of that of whites

The first Black pathology D'Souza addresses, on the surface, doesn't seem pathological at all, but deals with the premise that Blacks earn only 60 cents for every dollar a White person earns. Taken at face value, it seems that this is an obvious and unjust disparity in the American economy. However, upon closer scrutiny, D'Souza cites the following mitigating circumstances which are often ignored:

> Let us examine specifically the argument that if African Americans earn less than Whites, the income differential can be presumed to be the result of discrimination. Such logic is very familiar: in a similar vein, we hear that women earn fifty-nine cents for every dollar earned by a man, the insinuation being that sexism is responsible for the differential. Andrew Hacker presumes the existence of discrimination because "while Black Americans made up 12.1 percent of the tabulated population, they ended up with only 7.8 percent of the monetary pie." Yet as is the case with gender gaps, racial gaps in family earnings

between groups cannot be understood without considering relevant variables such as gender, age, geography, family structure, and most important, credentials, experience, and levels of skill. It proves nothing to point out that Black college graduates as a group earn less than White college graduates. Only if Black students attend the same colleges, take the same courses, and attain the same grade point average, would a group comparison of this sort make sense. Why is it reasonable to expect that Black students majoring in education with a C average at a community college should command incomes comparable with White students majoring in business with a B average at the University of Wisconsin or Cornell? (pp. 300–01).

Once again, in brilliant fashion, D'Souza shifts the focus away from the pretext of racism mythology, to the real problem, Black pathology. For example, another rational explanation for Blacks earning 60% of Whites is that a large percentage of working age and potentially marrying-type Black men, ages 18–35, are involved in some aspect of the prison system—prison, parole, probation. It doesn't take an economist to deduce that your *statistical* proportion of the "monetary pie," as Hacker calls it, will not match the your *numerical* population with such a high proportion of the active workforce having taken themselves out the job market altogether—in many instances, permanently. Liberal activists, in citing such statistics as the 40% disparity between the incomes of Whites and Blacks, conveniently omit many other significant variables which attribute to such economic aberrations as cited by D'Souza and other writers,— namely age, gender, geography, education, experience, family structure.

Black Pathology #2

The black unemployment rate is nearly double that of the whole nation

Most liberals and civil rights activists would contend that the above statement is true solely due to White racism. The presumption here is that if Whites (who presumably control the best jobs and determine who gets hired) would be fair and evenhanded to potential job applicants, Black and White unemployment would be about the same. Countering this assumption, D'Souza writes that, "Undoubtedly the main obstacle to the implementation of proportional representation in the workforce is the fact of large differences of developed ability and demonstrated performance among various ethnic and racial groups." Also, Black pathology must be factored into any equation seeking to understand why Black people are twice as likely as Whites to be unemployed. The level and security of one's employment, as D'Souza states, is inextricably linked to "developed ability" and "demonstrated performance." For example, Blacks in general score much lower on standardized tests than any other racial group in America. The tests include: the Scholastic Aptitude Test, National Assessment of Educational Progress, Law School Admission Test, Bar Exam, Graduate Management Admission Test, Graduate Record Exam, Doctoral Degrees Earned, Armed Forces Qualification Test and General Aptitude Test Battery (GATB), despite socio-economic factors (p. 309). Like them or not, these tests are the bridges from poverty and menial existence to the independent, well-paying, secure jobs of the middle-class. This great disparity in Black/White achievement levels on aptitude tests, lead Christopher Jencks to write:

When Black and White students take tests that measure vocabulary, reading comprehension, mathematical skill, or scientific information, blacks do much worse than whites. If employers valued educated workers mainly for their skills, Whites, would almost inevitably earn more than Blacks with the same amount of schooling (p. 301).

Other interesting facts about Black employment and unemployment D'Souza cites are:

- "Black women with college degrees earn more than White women with college degrees."
- The median age of U.S. citizens is 33; Mexicans, Puerto Ricans=under 25; American Indians=26; African Americans=28; white Americans=25; Jews, over 40. The premise being, the younger and less educated you are, the less likely it is that you will be employed.
- "50 percent of Blacks still live in the South."
- "Mexicans on average have larger families. Many African Americans live in single-parent families. Asian Americans have a higher rate of intact families than other minority groups, as well as the highest percentage of working members per family" (pp. 301–02).

Black Pathology #3

One third of Blacks are poor, compared with just over 10 percent of Whites

The myth about the majority of Blacks being poor is one of the most potent and often used weapons liberal activist groups use to coerce and extort more money from the federal government to fund their power base and to increase their political clout in the public domain. D'Souza cites statistics showing:

> As of 1994 only about one-third of blacks were poor; the rest were middle-class or better off. Approximately 16 percent of Black families currently earn more than $50,000, 27 percent earn between $25,000 and $50,000, 30 percent earn between, $10,000 and $25,000, and 26 percent earn under $10,000. What this means is that poor Blacks are now a minority of African Americans (pp. 239–240).

One of the most egregious and frequent injustices foisted upon economically poor Blacks by liberals and civil rights activists, has been how they have so shamelessly used the poor as poster children to fund large federal programs to remedy the plight of the poor, when most of the money goes into the pockets of the civil rights establishment and to federal bureaucrats—many of them disproportionately Black. University economist Walter Williams calls the civil rights establishment, "Poverty Pimps." Although this is an inflammatory malediction, it accurately represents the liberal approach to the poor. Williams sees the modern-day civil rights movement as pimps using their own people to extort money from the federal government to fund programs and schemes that are proven failures and that will only mire the poor into an ever-increasing depth of poverty. On this topic D'Souza writes:

> The civil rights establishment has a vested interest in the continuation of spectacular episodes of racism: these provide an important justification for continuing transfer payments to minority activists. (p. 238)

However, liberal civil rights activists realize that this money has a two-fold purpose: (1) it solidifies their position as the champions of the poor, while enlarging their coffers and political influence and; (2) federal largess guarantees civil rights activists that at least 25% of African Americans will remain dependant, poor, ignorant, and hopeless as their pimps concoct scheme after scheme to "help the poor," or to "help the children."

One of the often cited examples of how societal racism has been used to keep Blacks and other minorities poor has been the so-called redlining by banks and other lending institutions against making loans to them to obtain home mortgagees, or to start businesses. On this topic D'Souza writes:

> Although charges of lending discrimination have been around for years, going back to the redlining controversy of the 1960s, discrimination studies until recently have tended to be amateurish and inadequate, propelled to public attention by uncritical news reports. The problem with most of the studies was that they focused mainly on differences in rejection rates between Black and White applicants, without taking into account their levels of income but without considering other factors such as net worth, existing levels of debt, credit history, job stability, and size of down payment. Lenders consider all these factors, not just earnings, in approving credit applications. . . . White households have a median net worth of around $45,000 while Black households have a median net worth of only $4,200, less than one tenth that of whites. Since Black incomes have risen dramatically only during the last few decades, even Blacks and Whites who earn roughly the same amount often have vastly different levels of net worth. (pp. 279–280).

Black Pathology #4

One half of all black children live in poverty

This is a favorite statistic liberal activists love to trumpet to coerce and extort more money to support not the children, but their organizations allegedly setup to help the children. It is related to Pathology #3 because it deals with poverty, but specifically here it concerns organizations that help children out of poverty (which pulls at most people's heart strings). In actuality, these liberal activist children organizations are exploiting the poverty of children to extract more money from the federal government. Unlike Pathology # 3 where the economically poor are actually a minority within the Black community, here, because so many Black children are born illegitimate to immature or teenage mothers who are mostly unmarried, uneducated, poor, with little prospects for living a useful life, a disproportionate number of Black children are unnecessarily forced to live their young lives in poverty. However, various liberal children's organizations like The Childrens Defense Fund, of which First Lady Hillary Rodam Clinton and later Dr. Marion Wright Edelman, served as the previous president and current president, respectively, prefer to de-emphasize the pathological and aberrant behavior of the individual mother. Why? In most cases where a child is born illegitimate, it is because of the mother's promiscuity and willful ignorance. To liberal activists of a cultural relativist mind set, this type of analysis is viewed as "judgmental," "blaming the victim," "counterproductive," and inimical to finding "solutions." So liberals, in classic cultural relativist fashion, shift the root blame and causes of why one-half of all Black children live in poverty away from Black pathology—namely promiscuity, ignorance, and a greater susceptibility to and participation in criminal activity, to fanciful, sophistic sociological theories like the one popularized by Oscar Lewis' "culture of poverty." D'Souza writes:

> The traditional liberal view of why blacks are disproportionately poor may have developed a "culture of poverty" which contributed to an ethic of underachievement. Popularized by Oscar Lewis, the "culture of poverty" thesis held that poor people who frequently belong to minority groups develop attitudes and behaviors that are an adaptation to chronic joblessness and social immobility. The effect of these cultural patterns, however, is to exacerbate these conditions. Thus begins a vicious cycle of poverty and underachievement. (p. 454)

Once again liberal activists, by shifting the spotlight away from the people who are most responsible for their own predicament, are impotent to offer any substantive remedies for eradicating poverty among children. For as long as liberal activists, and the organizations they control, continue to benefit from federal largess in the name of ending poverty among Black children, while irrationally ignoring the underlying root causes of Black poverty—promiscuity, ignorance, and criminal tendencies of their parents, the rate of poverty among Black children will continue to escalate.

Black Pathology #5

The infant mortality rate for blacks is more than double that of whites

This diabolical statistic should come as no surprise to a race who has allowed it's own people for the past thirty-five years to be victimized by the previously cited four pathologies.

What would you expect??!! Alcoholism, illegitimacy, rampant promiscuity, teenage pregnancy, drug abuse, smoking, lack of prenatal care—all contributing to low birth weight babies which are at an increased risk of death before their first birthday. This must be the inevitable result to those who so cavalierly engage in such self-destructive practices as these. Although D'Souza says little explicitly in his book about infant mortality, he cites such a wealth of information about its underlying causes that it is easy for the reader to understand why the infant mortality rate of Black people is double that of Whites. The common scenario is this: A young Black adolescent girl living in the inner-city. She is most likely living in a chaotic family headed by her single, poorly educated mother, who has several children by perhaps two to three different fathers. Add to this an incessant exposure to smoking, alcoholism, sexual abuse (possibly by mother's boyfriend), drug abuse, a high crime, and low achievement environment. The young girl, following the example of her forefathers, gets pregnant while still a child herself. There is no shame. She may even be given a party by her mother or friends to celebrate this event. Functioning in this environment of promiscuity, ignorance, and criminality (i.e., having sex with an underage minor is considered statutory rape in most states), she gets little or no prenatal care, leading to a baby having low birth weight, premature, diseased, and having life-long physical and/or mental impairments. All of the factors will greatly increase the risk of death before the baby's first birthday—if the poor child makes it that far.

Liberal activists, knowing of these dire statistics, distort and reverse them, and use their cultural relativist ideology as the primary reason to *continue* funding the very programs that either contributed to, fostered, enabled, or caused the very pathologies that lead to such a high infant mortality rate among Black children in the first place. Ironically, this is the same philosophy Hitler used to kill the Jews during World War II. Hitler built crematoriums to deal with his "Jewish problem." As the Allies discovered his atrocities, Hitler had a new problem (possible interference by the Allies). He remedied his new problem by building more crematoriums to kill more Jews faster and more efficiently, and when this didn't work as effectively as he had hoped, the Nazi's simply shot them and dumped the bodies in mass graves that the Jews were forced to dig themselves. Hitler even forbade his generals from using the trains to send food, supplies, and fresh soldiers to the front because he said, "I must have those trains for the Jews" (i.e., to transport the Jew to the crematoriums). Such is the slippery slope of cultural relativism. Its adherents become trapped in their own maniacal philosophy, destroying or severely damaging the very lives of the people they are supposedly trying to help.

Black Pathology #6

The proportion of black male high school graduates who go on to college is lower today than in 1975

Here, D'Souza shows a keen awareness of the counter-intuitive and destructive logic of cultural relativism. Since President Lyndon Johnson's "war on poverty" programs of the 1960s, several trillions of dollars have been directed to ridding America of poverty and improving educational standards, especially of Black Americans. Instead, the law of unintended circumstances has occurred, and we have many more poor children and plummeting SAT scores among Black high school students than ever before. Why is this so? As stated earlier, in America, we have more Black men in some aspect of the criminal justice system than in college. This increase in the incarceration rate of Black males, especially since the 1980s, coupled with a very high crime rate in most Black communities, and the general increase in overt pathological behavior by African Americans, is a direct correlation of why in America there are more Black males in prison today than in college and why fewer Black male high school graduates go on to college today than in 1975. In the face of this crisis, one might expect a vigorous campaign to improve vocabulary skills, clarity of expression, numerical facility, and general academic standards among African Americans. Instead, quite the opposite has occurred. D'Souza writes:

> A large proportion of the African American population is illiterate, many adults cannot read beyond the fourth-grade level, the performance of blacks in school lags behind that of whites on every measure of performance, only about one third of Blacks who go to college graduate within six years. African Americans seem woefully lacking in the skills needed to compete effectively in a multiracial society, instead many students seem to have adopted, with the approval of their elders and civil rights leaders, a hostile stance toward the values of the White world, including the values of scholarship and study. Among some Blacks, "getting ignorant" is considered a virtue and a source of self-esteem. Indeed several studies have shown, contrary to popular wisdom, that the self-esteem of young Black males is higher than that of any other group. Apparently those who do not value educational success do not feel bad when they fail at something they don't care about. (p. 499)

Please allow me at this point to chronicle a personal experience of mine related to the above topic. Before I went to law school, I taught instrumental music in the Detroit Public School system for several years. The last grade level I taught was middle school kids (ages 12–15). During my tenure in this system, I daily witnessed a lynch mob mentality among the students in my class and throughout the school. Out of over one hundred students, I had about three to five students that really wanted to learn. I remind you that since instrumental music was an "elective" class, to be accepted, the students had to have an A or B grade point average. So presumably, I had the cream of the crop from this school. The several high achieving students I had were constantly threatened and harassed by their peers. One girl who played the alto sax was one of the few students that owned her instrument. She was my smartest and most conscientious student. Unfortunately, the students were so jealous of her that someone stole her saxophone from my music room. This act of thievery totally demoralized her, and within a few weeks, I could see signs of her openly "getting ignorant" towards me in order to be more accepted by her peers. Needless to say, her budding musical talent waned. The crab bucket syndrome that D'Souza writes about would apply to this situation.

D'Souza notes a societal phenomenon in the Black community called the "crab bucket syndrome." The crab bucket syndrome is where you have a bucket full of crabs, all desperately trying to get out, but as each crab makes his way to the top of the bucket, the other crabs reflexively pull him down (to dinner). This is exactly what occurred to my prize pupil. While she was at the top of probable musical success, her peers pulled her down to rebellion and academic failure. However, on a brighter note, I was able to secure summer music camp scholarships for four students who really wanted to succeed in music, and I have since heard that one of my former pupils from this school received a full music scholarship to study percussion instruments at Michigan State University! I can only hope that my short tenure in the Detroit Public School system has helped those students who had "an ear to hear." On this topic, D'Souza chronicles stories of Black students caught in the labyrinth of whether to act dumb and please their Black peers, or to seek after academic excellence and suffer the wrath of their fellow students. D'Souza cites such terms used against them as: "Wiggers," "acting white," and the heart-wrenching story of a young Black academician, caught in a societal purgatory desperately confessed: "We're not accepted by the White people because they think we're not smart enough. We're not accepted by Black people because they think we're too smart" (pp. 500–01).

Black Pathology #7

More young black males are in prison than in college

Proportional representation is a constant mantra of liberal activists as their way of proving that affirmative action is being implemented correctly in the work place or in university admissions policy. However, when the topic shifts from school or workplace minority representation to prison minority representation, unfortunately, the Black male is extremely over-represented. D'Souza cites a number of statistics to bolster his point:

> Although Blacks make up 12 percent of the national population, they comprise almost 50 percent of the prison population. Yet according to Uniform Crime Reports, which are data published annually by the FBI, Blacks comprise 39 percent of those arrested for aggravated assault, 42 percent of those arrested for weapons possession, 43 percent of those arrested for rape, 55 percent of those arrested for murder, and 61 percent of those arrested for robbery. (p. 260)

Liberal activists like to attribute such damning statistics to White racism or unfair discrimination in the criminal justice system. However, D'Souza further notes:

> Even discounting the possibility of some racial bias in criminal arrests, it seems clear that the average Black person is between three and six times more likely to be arrested for a crime than the average White person. To use the logic of proportional representation, blacks are vastly over represented among criminals in America today.... The overwhelming majority of crimes of robbery, mugging, sexual assault, and murder are perpetrated by men. There are very few elderly people arrested for committing those offenses. (p. 260)

Criminologist state that the majority of crimes nationwide are committed by the same 6 percent of the criminal population. Black males, between the ages 18–35, are the primary age range that most chronic criminal behavior occur. D'Souza writes that the data shows that young males between the ages of eighteen and thirty-five make up the segment within the African American community that is largely responsible for the Black crime rate. "This group," political scientist James Q. Wilson says, "commits a larger fraction of violent crimes than any segment of the national population." So in conclusion, we see that a very large number of Black men in the prime of their lives, instead of learning to secure regular employment, improving their intellectual abilities, and solidifying their educational opportunities so that they can be productive citizens, fathers, and role-models, are serving as the foot soldiers to the perpetuation of cultural genocide in the Black community, and assuring that America remains the most dangerous place on earth to live.

Black Pathology #8

Homicide is the leading cause of death for black males between the ages of fifteen and thirty-four

Much ink has been spilled about the epidemic crime rate in the Black community, and how homicide is the leading cause of death among Black youth. However, D'Souza's approach in citing the usual grim statistics are inextricably linked to the underlying sin, largely ignored by Black leadership, which is a common refrain throughout his book. The primary problem of African Americans isn't racism, but promiscuity, ignorance, and CRIME. D'Souza writes:

> Violence has now become a tragic defining feature of life in the Black underclass. African Americans in this group seem divided into two factions: perpetrators, and potential victims. Indeed violence unleased by Blacks seems to have reached a point where it threatens the future of the African American community and the stability of society as a whole.
> - In 1992, the violent crime rate for blacks was the highest ever recorded.
> - That same year, almost half of all murder victims were African American. Ninety-four percent of murdered Blacks were killed by other Blacks.
> - Black males are about twice as likely as White males to be victims of robbery, theft, and aggravated assault, and seven times more likely to be victims of murder.
> - In the District of Columbia, Black residents are more likely to be killed than are people in war-torn regions, such as Northern Ireland and the Middle East.
> - Partly as a consequence of Black crime, American crime rates are the highest in the industrialized world (p. 503).

D'Souza cites these statistics not to show how irredeemable Black people are, but how woefully deplorable, inadequate, and irresponsible society's attempts have been at remedying these destructible pathologies. While liberal activists continue to throw money at the problem, thirty years and over 5 trillion dollars later, government largess has repeatedly proven a patent failure to substantively improve Black developed ability and demonstrated performance levels to any significant degree. All but the willfully blind would agree that a Black person today is less likely to be killed by the Governor George Wallaces or Bull Connors of the world thirty years ago, than by your next-door neighbor who you had an argument with during a street basketball game in the 1990s.

The fact that more Black men in America between the ages of 18–35 are in prison than in college, makes it easy to see why the Black homicide rate for this age group is so astronomically high. This at-risk, or criminally-prone, age range has lead the frontal assault in systematically decimating the communities of their own Black people over the last thirty-five years despite a steady increase in the economic status of Blacks as a whole. What is the civil rights activist's response to this dire situation? Yell racism at every turn and demand more hush money from the federal government (i.e., taxpayers). In the meantime, the prison industry is the fastest growing sector of the American economy for the past ten years due to the criminally-prone age group of Black males who are fatherless, uneducated, undisciplined, and very, very angry.

Black Pathology #9

Although African Americans make up 12 percent of the population, they account for more than 35 percent of all AIDS cases

AIDS, as well as other sexually transmitted diseases (STDs), affect on the Black community is one of the saddest, tragic, but predictable, outgrowths of the cultural relativist philosophy. By now the reader should understand that pathological behavior doesn't exist in a vacuum, but is related to other pathologies and has a domino effect. Whether it is high school drop out rates, crime, fatherless households, STDs, drug abuse, or family violence, these pathologies are inextricably linked together—they feed, complement, and nurture one another. Black people aren't unique to these pathologies. They are disproportionately susceptible to these destructible behaviors because of their approach (or lack thereof) in seriously confronting these problems causes them to exacerbate, creating the cultural and societal chaos we have in the Black community today. For example, D'Souza writes:

> According to the Center for Disease Control, the AIDS rate among African Americans is about three times higher than among the U.S. population overall, and more than 50 percent of children with AIDS are Black. Part of the reason for this is the common practice of poor Black women exchanging sex for drugs . . . sexual abuse, physical child abuse, and family violence are arguably among the most serious social problems in the black community. (p. 515)

Here, one can see the pathological domino effect AIDS has on the Black community which, has spread among them in Biblical proportions. D'Souza links the high incidence of AIDS among African Americans largely to promiscuous sex by drug addicted women who sell their bodies for drugs. Of course each sex act increases the chances of spreading the disease to others geometrically, so the men (primarily Black) do not leave unscathed, but continue to spread the disease to their multiple sex partners, sometimes for as long as a decade or more before realizing that they have the disease. Lately, these women have even prostituted their own children to obtain drugs for their habit. Therefore, we see in this tragic AIDS scenario—from one sin (lack of discipline), the Black woman falls prey to drug usage, leading to incessant promiscuity as her need for drugs increases. In the meantime, the effects of illicit drug usage and promiscuous sex take their toll on her body. As she becomes more desperate for drugs, and less physically desirable, she may willingly use her innocent son or daughter to perform sexually for her customers to support her drug habit, thus subjecting her and her children to a variety of deadly diseases including AIDS. Sexual abuse, physical child abuse, and family violence continue to make African Americans over 300% more likely to get AIDS than any other race. The liberal response is once again predictable. Give us more federal funds to fight AIDS and educate the public about how to avoid infection. (N.B. that liberals don't want federal funds to fight illegitimacy, promiscuity, or parental neglect). One thing that is important to understand is that when liberals say "educate," what they mean is *indoctrinate*—to create in the public mind a cultural relativist mind-set so that those who control the levers of power will make others conform to their view and remedies to social problems, which as I have chronicled in this review, has tragically exacerbated these problems.

Black Pathology #10

The life expectancy of black men is sixty-five years, a rate lower than any other group in America and comparable to that of some Third World countries

The tenth pathology afflicting the Black community that D'Souza cites is life expectancy, which is linked to the previous nine pathologies in that they all directly or indirectly have a very serious adverse impact on one's quantity and quality of life. Is it rational for a racial subgroup of men engaging in numerous forms of highly destructive and life-threatening behavioral practices, such as promiscuous sex, excessive violence, and little interest in education, to expect longevity? What is rather shocking is the fact that the life expectancy for a Black man in America in 1997 is lower than that of the poorest of countries of the Third World. D'Souza writes, "The life expectancy of Black men in central Harlem is shorter than that of men in Bangladesh" (p. 503). And:

> One of the main sources for this violence is the African American cultural orientation of the "bad nigger." . . . this outlaw figure has been a revered archetype since slavery. In the view of many blacks, his very badness becomes a symbol of heroic resistance to white oppression. . . . Most African American scholars simply refuse to acknowledge the pathology of violence in the Black underclass, apparently convinced that Black criminals as well as their targets are both victims: the real culprit is societal racism. (pp. 503–04)

Why is this so? Certainly a man born in a miserably poor country such as Bangladesh where the average annual income is less than $100.00, and without access to government welfare programs and federal largess, couldn't be expected to live longer than a poor Black man born in Harlem? Because even though he is poor and lives in an economically depressed environment—he lives in America, the richest country in the history of mankind, where the opportunities to break the shackles of poverty are infinitely more available to him than for his brother in a Third World country like Bangladesh or Haiti. D'Souza cites the glorification of the "bad nigger" archetype as a possible explanation for the high tolerance for violence in the Black community, which adversely diminishes the life expectancy of the Black man who in many cases is either the perpetrator or victim of life extinguishing behaviors.

Black Pathology #11

Nearly 50 percent of all African American families are headed by single women

Perhaps never in the history of civilization has a race of people had such a high percentage of its families headed by women. The consequences in the Black community have been devastating, fostering generation after generation of fatherless, loveless, angry young Black males, increasingly ambivalent to any authority and prone to criminal behavior. Add to this a new generation of young, educated, Black females who use their newfound feminists philosophy (which is also a relativist doctrine) as a license to be promiscuous and hostile to the traditional family values that her forefathers respected only a generation ago. However, the twin sister of the pathological Black male (i.e., Bad Nigger) is the ubiquitous, unmarried, uneducated Black female, laden with numerous illegitimate children, living in the squalor of an inner-city ghetto, surrounded by depredation, violence, and ignorance. It is she who has been the incubator to several generations of progeny who are irredeemable law breakers and blights to society. D'Souza writes:

> . . . Robert Taylor Homes and Cabrini Green [are] the largest and second largest housing projects in Chicago. William Julius Wilson reports that in Robert Taylor Homes, with a virtually all-black population of twenty thousand, 90 percent of households are headed by women, and 81 percent are on welfare. Although less than 1 percent of Chicago's population lives in the project, residents commit about 10 percent of all assaults, rapes, and murders in the city. In Cabrini Green, with a population of fourteen thousand, once again the single-parent families numbered about 90 percent, and 70 percent were supported by welfare. Within a few weeks, Wilson counted ten murders and thirty-five woundings by gunshot in that project. (p. 515)

What is the liberal activist's answer to this deplorable tragedy? More federal aid, education, and job programs; stronger gun control legislation. They protest, "Don't tear down the Robert Taylor Homes or Cabrini Green, but build more of the same." In response, the liberal press offers little or no challenge to these absurd solutions, but merely apes whatever liberal activists like Jesse Jackson or the local, big-city politicians tell them to write on this issue. The end result: keep project residents and the underclass poor, dumb, dependant on government largess, and forever damned to the ghetto. Any truly viable ideas or programs proposed that are contrary to their cultural relativist ideology, are viciously deposed by the self-appointed jailers of the poor—the race merchants and the poverty pimps. D'Souza addresses the link of single parenthood and poverty by citing a famous study:

In an authoritative review, *Single Mothers and Their Children,* Irwin Garfinkel and Sara McLanahan show that single parenthood is closely correlated with, and contributes to, poverty and lack of opportunity. Garfinkel and McLanahan point out that mother-only families are five times more likely than two-parent families to be poor. Indeed, of all Black families with children below the poverty line in 1991, 83 percent were single-parent households headed by a woman; only 13 percent were married-couple families. Moreover, daughters of single-parent families are more likely to have illegitimate children themselves. . . . The scientific evidence suggests that children who grow up in families headed by single mothers do worse as adults than children who grow up in families with two parents. (p. 516)

With such an overwhelming weight of authority against single parents and in favor of a two-parent family as the ideal standard, economically, psychologically, and socially, liberal activists in general, and feminists in particular, continue to trumpet the cultural relativist propaganda which state otherwise. Feminists hold that a single mother can be "just as good" a parent to a child as the traditional two-parent home. To feminists, "their career," is their god, their primary goal, their sole driving force, and they regard any ideas to the contrary as a threat to keeping women tied down to the family and unavailable to pursue high-profile and influential career opportunities.

Black Pathology #12

More than 65 percent of black children born each year are illegitimate

The twelfth and final pathology D'Souza cites that African

Americans need to seriously address is the problem of exceedingly high rates of illegitimacy, which is over 65% nationally and in some inner-cities like my home town of Detroit, MI, as high as 80%. D'Souza writes, "After remaining relatively stable for the first half of this century, the Black illegitimacy rate seems to have reached a critical mass during the 1960's and simply exploded since then" (p.516). He further states:

> Whites too have a problem with illegitimacy, but to date the White norm remains the two-parent household. What is significant in the African American community is that illegitimacy is normalized, both statistically and morally. Studies have shown that the Black community is more tolerant about births for unwed mothers than society at large. (p. 515)

Illegitimate children have always been a part of American society, however, never at such high percentages and in such great numbers in a single race. On this topic, D'Souza writes:

> Perhaps the most serious of African American pathologies—no less serious than violence—is the routinization of illegitimacy as a way of life. The bastardization of Black America is confirmed by the fact that nearly 70 percent of young Black children born in the United States today are illegitimate, compared with 22 percent of white children. . . . Almost 95 percent of Black teen mothers are unmarried, compared with 55 percent of their White peers. Illegitimacy and single-parent households are not exclusive characteristics of the Black underclass: College-educated African American women have children outside of marriage at a rate about seven to eight times higher than that of college-educated White women . . . an almost complete separation of marriage and childbearing among African Americans. (pp. 514–515)

Once again, the specter of cultural relativism is the driving ideology behind both in the support of such pathologies and in actively fighting against and undermining any substantive remedies. For example, the general view regarding illegitimacy of most liberal activist and so-called "children advocate" groups are that there is no such thing as an illegitimate child. To liberals, schooled in the philosophy of cultural relativism, the very word itself sounds "religious" or "judgmental," and liberals have little use for Biblical references. Secondly, activists contend that people using such terms are pushing their Eurocentric or Western moral values on people who don't share them. On the first point, for anyone to believe that no child should be considered illegitimate, completely ignores 6,000 years of civilizational development to the contrary, whereby all civilized cultures throughout history (East and West) put a premium on virginity and against illegitimacy, because even the ancients understood the vital need to maintain structural integrity of the family as the key to maintaining civilizational existence. On the second point, the anti-Western, anti-Eurocentric argument liberals claim Blacks are revolting against by the permissive lifestyles they adopt, belie the true origins of all morality—Biblical theism. No matter what culture you are from, you will find the moral code of the world evidenced in that society, namely the Ten Commandments. The Eurocentric argument is a red herring and a pretext to justify promiscuous behavior. Therefore, favoring legitimacy can be traced in the historical texts of most cultures through their folksongs, religion, and poetry. Why is this so? D'Souza quotes anthropologist David Murray, "No community can survive over the long term without the family as a viable institution." Murray argues that, "marriage is a productive institution because it makes relatives out of strangers. It provides a matrix of support for children that no other structure can provide" (p. 515).

Conclusion

In summary, D'Souza's primary thesis in his book, *The End of Racism,* is not to postulate that racism no longer exists (a false charge made by many reviewers of his book in the past). D'Souza consistently acknowledges racism, but issues the sobering challenge to Black people: So what! He acknowledges that African American's have been the most frequent victims of racism and discriminatory practices, but also informs us that Black people have been most likely to be used by liberal demagogues to continue to perpetuate the racism mythologies discussed in Part I of this review essay. D'Souza's sobering, but cathartic remedy is to break free from the shackles of victimhood and silly cliches like—"the White man,"or "Racism in America" are the reasons why Black people have so many problems, and to awake to a new, bold, fresh and objective approach in dealing with racism. Blacks must believe and teach their children to believe that despite racism and discrimination, both real and imagined, I can and will achieve a successful and fulfilling life by: (1) ridding myself of self-destructive tendencies in my own character—promiscuity, ignorance, crime; (2) demand that others in the African American community uphold removal of the same; and, (3) hold to a total rejection of the classical liberal activists' view that White racism is the cause of Black problems. On this point D'Souza offers the following sublime and poignant prophecy:

> Liberals should stop listening to the fashionable prophets of despair who once led the nation nobly and admirably, but who have now become reactionary fogies. So committed are they to the paradigm of racial struggle that they are unable to see and seize new opportunities. Civil rights mythographers are fond of painting Martin Luther King as the Moses of the movement, who, in his own prophetic words, would never reach the

Promised Land. What has not been noted is the obvious corollary to this elegant myth: like the Hebrews whom Moses shepherded through the desert for 40 years, today's civil rights leaders are too steeped in the mentality of Egypt to be admitted into Canaan; they may have to die out altogether before a new generation can arise to claim the fruits of their long and largely successful struggle against racial discrimination in this country. These bitter and bewildered old idolaters should invest their earnings from racial soothsaying and take a well-earned retirement from the civil rights debate. (p. 553)

This will be one of the greatest challenges for African Americans as we approach the twenty-first century. The question is, will we remain in the muck and mire as slaves to an impersonal, Leviathan government bureaucracy? Or will we pull ourselves up by the bootstraps as did our forefathers, other races, and immigrants to America for over 300 years? purging ourselves of our base natures, paganisms, and primitive practices learned in our old cultures, confronting and dispelling myths, and joining the new millennia as productive, upstanding, and self-reliant participants in the universal pantheon of nations.